SAVIORS OF THE CHILDREN

*

ERIC ANTHONY MOUZON

Dedicated to the memory of Heriberto "Eddie" Concepcion.
It is you whom I think of now and always. Rest in Heavenly peace, *compadre*.

This book was written also in dedication to all of the Child Protective Services workers of America. CPS workers are the true backbone of family and social services. So much has been said and written about the plights of families and others who have had CPS involvement in their lives, for a variety of reasons--real, imagined, or otherwise.

The core values in CPS work are *Ethics, Responsibility, Integrity, Competence,* and most essential, *Empathy.* In most (if not all) instances, CPS workers must bring a sense of understanding and support to the families they serve; they must set aside their personal feelings and biases while dealing with parents, children, and others--yet also be able to detach themselves at the end of the day. Many a worker will get burned out, and it will show in their tone, demeanor, and body language.

Never take the job home! Sometimes this is easier said than done. In my career as a CPS worker, many a night I've lain awake, thinking of young "Joey", wondering if he's okay in his placement, or of "Maryann" (these are not real names) and her mom, hoping that they are keeping the peace in their constant battles, which had evolved into physical confrontation.

While this is (per my disclaimer) a work of

fictitious characters, there have been some actual real happenings which I've purposely omitted. In one state, two CPS workers were shot dead upon approaching a family home to speak with the parent; in another, a CPS worker was brutally stabbed and left for dead. There are countless incidents across the nation concerning workers' safety. CPS workers have had guns drawn, knives pointed, dogs sicced on them.

And then there is the mountain of paperwork! One client at a time, one case at a time. The court reviews, the regular home visitations, scheduling supervised visits between the parent(s) and child(ren) who are in placement out of the family home. Again, for a variety of reasons. Are the parents acting/speaking appropriately? Is the monitoring worker noticing (and noting) everything going on during the visit? Is the parent (if there is substance-abuse history) showing up for his/her scheduled screenings? Does he/she comply with court-ordered stipulations?

And to add to this, knowing and understanding the child's history--medical, educational, and other. How is the child doing in school? Are his/her grades up to par? Is he/she attending school every day?

Did the child come from a home infested

with head lice, bed bugs, or other contagious afflictions? Asthma and allergies also play a huge factor--does he or she have a nebulizer? Allergic to certain foods or other? Does/did the child have Strep? MRSA? (*Methicillin-Resistant Staphylococcus Aureus,* pronounced in acronym as MERSA) or other contagious illness.

Now multiply this by ten. Each case is unique. Obviously, not all cases will have everything mentioned above, but as a case worker you have to treat each differently, on an individual basis. The Smith family (again, not real names) will not have the same issues as those of Mrs. Jones and her children. And in the meantime, you're shackled to paperwork in attempting to reunify Mr. and Mrs. Rodriguez with their child. Moreover, another parent has been arrested and may be facing significant time in jail, while yet another parent has just been hospitalized--this parent had been in a serious accident or was taken ill.

And in yet another, one of your young clients has just been arrested and is sitting in the juvenile detention facility. Or after a big fight in the home, was kicked out of the house by their parent. So now, that CPS worker has ten cases that he or she is overseeing, five of whom needing priority attention!

This is to emphatically not to discourage anyone from becoming a Child Protective Services worker in any way, shape, or form! It is, rather, a rewarding job. It should go without saying that the job of CPS is not akin to that of a Wall Street investment banker--the pay is low, the morale is borderline, the stress is super-high--but at the end of the day, a CPS worker will know and understand that he or she has done the absolute best thing for the safety of the child and family.

Children are a heritage from the Lord, offspring a reward from Him. Like arrows in the hands of a warrior are children born in one's youth. Blessed is the man whose quiver is full of them. They will not be put to shame when they contend with their opponents in court. -Psalm 127: 3-5

DISCLAIMER

The happenings in this book may or may not be true. The characters within are fictitious. The author takes no responsibility for any events that may or may not have occurred in the lives of Child Protective Services workers, their superiors, client families, or other. Any resemblances to any events, or those to any person or persons living or dead is purely coincidental.

"Give it here!"

It wasn't a request; it was a command. What other way did the kid know to speak? He had never been asked, he'd been *told* to do things.

Nick looked at him--a frozen, stern glare--to indicate that the young man needed to adjust his way of speaking. Not reading his expression, the youngster repeated his order, but finally noticing the older man's look, added a not-so-meaningful *"please."*

The "it" was a portable MP3 player that was held for security while the young man--a Division client--was appearing before a judge.

The scenario was the corridor outside of the courtroom. The purpose of the court appearance was to answer to traffic charges: the young man--Jeremy by name--was picked up for driving without a license and running a stop sign. The officer, noticing Jeremy's youthful appearance--he was sixteen, but looked much younger--had pulled him over and Jeremy, with no love for the cops, proceeded to curse the officer and call him names. Such resulted in his next ride being in the back of the police car.

Jeremy was a stocky youngster with brown hair and hazel eyes. He had no problem attracting girls, could be quite charming, and though not proven or verified, no one doubted that he had had a few sexual encounters with some of the girls he charmed.

He came from what was considered a "good area", meaning a quiet suburban town with little or no crime. In spite of such, Jeremy chose to hang out with the "bad boys", thus acting as one. He talked tough, acted tough, used foul language and was defiant.

Nick knew that Jeremy in reality was a loudmouthed punk who couldn't fight his way out of wet paper bag. Now the punk was demanding his MP3 back.

"You know way better than to talk to me that way!" Nick said in a hard voice, "I'm not one of your little 'homies' and you best check that attitude at the door!"

Seeing that the Division worker meant business, the young man backed down. His shoulders dropped and expression softened, he pleaded with his eyes and after a few seconds, Nick handed the boy his device. *From a tiger to a kitten*, Nick thought to himself.

Walking to the court cashier's window, Nick arranged for Jeremy to pay his fines on or by a certain time. Having been bailed out of jail by his mother, whose car he had taken, Jeremy discovered that the bail money would be used toward the cost of the fines. However, he owed an extra $200 to the court, plus court costs. It was agreed that the balance would be paid within the next two weeks.

Finished with court, Nick drove Jeremy home and returned to the Division office.

Nick Donovan was a tall, lanky man approaching his mid-forties with a friendly, boyish demeanor. He had worked in Social Services for fifteen years, six of whom for the State Child Protective Services as an Assistant Family Service Worker. Though not having any current cases per se, he assisted with numerous other cases in his unit. He spent much of his working hours on the road, transporting clients and families to appointments, visitations, and other essential functions; he also did some home visits and supervised family visits--either in the office or out in the field--and when not out of the office, prepared documents for school, medical, and police background checks for clients, parents, family members and potential caregivers.

Nick liked his job, and the people he worked with, but to many "outsiders" (people not working in CPS) he and other workers were sometimes treated as if they had leprosy. "Oh, you're here to take my kids away!" some would yell at him. *Baby snatchers!* others called him. At one point, he was compared to the people who took the Lindbergh baby! This remark hit a nerve, and although he wanted to retaliate, Nick kept his composure.

Time and again, Nick had done his best to show empathy for the many families with whom he worked. He would speak with the young clients and families on a one-to-one basis, his manner calm and disarming. This way, he got to know and understand their strengths and weaknesses, sometimes more so than the supervisors and administrators. At one point early in his career, this was frowned upon by the then-LOM (Local office Manager), who called nick into her office, and with Nick's own Unit Supervisor present, tried to order him *not* to speak with any clients.

Protesting this order, Nick fought back. "If you don't want me talking with anyone," he stated tartly, "then don't have me supervising any visits or going to any family homes! I got a job to do, and I'll be damned if you or anyone else's gonna tell me how to do it!"

There was stress in the job, and lots of it.

Prior to coming to the Division, Nick had heard stories of workers getting burned out. One worker had actually committed suicide, it was told, overwhelmed by the heavy caseloads. Nick had seen workers walk out of the office in tears; two workers in another Local Office suffered nervous breakdowns;

another suffered a heart attack, taking early disability retirement.

Nick had vowed that he would never let it happen to him. He worked long hours at times, getting up as early as 5 a.m. to pick up a client, ending his work day sometimes as late as Midnight. He told himself that no matter what, he would take time off for himself when needed. Luckily, for him, he had a lady who understood what he did for a living, and was compassionate. She loved him and showed her boundless concern.

****

"Can you buddy me on an MVR?"

Arlene Rollins was asking Paulette Dahl to assist on a family visit at a home--a Minimum Visitation Requirement, or MVR.

Arlene, a Family Service Specialist Trainee, had been with the Division for just over eighteen months; her potential "buddy", Paulette, was a Family Service Specialist 2 with four years on the job and a caseload that kept her beyond occupied. Both women were assigned to the Adolescent unit.

"Need to finish this court crap," Paulette said, "But when's your MVR?"

"At four," said Arlene, "It's the Peters case."

"Ohhhh…" Paulette moaned. The Peters case was one with a family of six, a single mom, four teenagers and a pre-teen. Two of the older teens were incarcerated--one in a county juvenile detention facility, the other in the state school for boys. A third teenager--a 15-year-old--was on probation for possession of stolen property.

"Back to the brick jungle!" Paulette said dispiritedly, "Not that I care, but just dodgin' the gauntlet there…" The Peters family lived in a housing project and the complex was riddled with drugs, drug dealers, gangs, and flying bullets. No ordinary person even thought of venturing there in broad daylight, let alone after dark!

"Run it by Bryan and we'll run over, get it done fast and get ourselves the hell outa Dodge!" said Paulette. Arlene nodded and headed over to their Unit Supervisor.

Bryan Taylor was a man of medium height and build in his late forties. He had started with the Division some twenty years prior, worked his way up and now headed the LO's

Adolescent unit. Given the astronomical record of court cases in the unit--family and criminal--it seemed that he spent more time in court than in the office; he was in constant contact with the DAG (Deputy Attorney General) and the Litigation unit, both within the LO.

"Just watch your asses over there," he told Arlene, "You can never be too careful."

The two workers signed out a State vehicle from the LO car coordinator and drove to the Malcolm X Housing Projects. Getting out of the car, both women made it a point to note their surroundings as they shut and locked the doors.

They also made a mental note of their appearance: casual but businesslike, flat-heeled shoes, walking not aimlessly but definitely not carelessly.

Ms. Peters lived on the 5th floor of one of the buildings. Neither Arlene nor Paulette were fond of taking the elevator--who knows who, or what, could be lurking in the elevator, but they sure as hell were not about to climb five flights of stairs!

They got off the elevator to the loud, booming noise of rap music blaring from a neighboring apartment. Arlene banged the knocker of Apartment 5C loudly, hoping that her banging could be heard over the noise.

"Who is it?" came a voice from the other side of the door. Arlene identified herself and the sound of deadbolt locks could be heard being disengaged.

The door was opened by Ms. Peters' youngest son. He was a thin, almost frail-looking boy with close-cropped hair and wearing a stained T-shirt, faded pants that seemed two sizes too big hanging halfway down his buttocks, and a pair of worn LeBron James basketball shoes on his feet. He opened wider to let the workers in. "My ma be out in a minute." he said, his voice cautious.

The apartment smelled of a combination of cigarette smoke and body odor. Wrinkling their noses, the workers walked into the living room to await their host.

Ms. Peters was a short, thin woman dressed in a worn-out blouse and shorts. She greeted the workers cordially and when she smiled, Paulette noticed, her mouth displayed a set of rotting teeth. *Guess she's never used a toothbrush,* Paulette thought.

Ms. Peters asked the workers to sit. The furniture looked as if it had been bought at a rummage sale. "Wanted to know how things are with you." Arlene began, "Any changes in Tamir and how he's doing with you." Tamir was the young man who had opened the door.

"He back in school now," Ms. Peters stated,

"His teacher sayin' that he tryin' to learn, but it's real slow wit' him. I been tryin' ta help him wit' his homework an' stuff, but some a' dat stuff they be givin' him....whooo-eee! They never gave me none a' dat stuff in school when I was his age!"

Arlene had gone over the school files. Tamir Peters, age 12, was a bright young man with a potentially positive outlook. However, his academic level was at that of a second-grader and he was still learning to add and subtract, while other boys his age had mastered the multiplication and division tables. It hardly helped that the so-called role models in his life were the local drug dealers who wore the fancy clothes, sported heavy jewelry, and drove the flashy cars. That two of his older brothers were locked up hardly even fazed him.

Ms. Peters was trying her best, so she claimed. She had a past arrest record for drugs and had been under the influence of drugs and alcohol while the children were in her care. A couple of years prior, on a complaint call, a DODD was ordered and the children were taken and placed in resource care. She had attended all of her court-ordered programs, submitted to random urine screenings, and gotten clean and sober. All but two of her children were reunified--the two older boys were arrested while in resource care and it was hoped that they would be reunified upon release.

Observing the mom closely, Paulette noticed a strong smell of Listerine on her breath. While her demeanor was friendly, Ms. Peters constantly averted her eyes, made furtive body movements and gestured heavily with her hands while speaking. The worker made a mental note to have the mom screened.

"I'm still fightin' wit' SSI to get my check," she said, rocking slowly back and forth in her chair, "I need food…I got a $400 light bill….PSE&G gettin' ready ta shut my lights off…"

A small crashing sound came from outside, but little attention was paid to it. Probably a car accident, thought everyone. Arlene asked if she and Paulette could check the house, and Ms. Peters affirmed.

Paulette checked the bedrooms. The kids' rooms were not spotless, but were not outright filthy either. There were clothes hanging off a closet door, a PlayStation on the bureau, and a small mound of dirty clothes in a corner. "I need to do the kids' laundry," claimed Ms. Peters upon notice.

The bathroom sink had rust stains, but the water from the tap was free-flowing. The toilet flushed, and there were a few hygiene items scattered about--a tube of toothpaste, two bars of soap, a can of Right Guard. The wall tiles were mildewy, and could benefit from a can of Lysol--in fact, the *whole apartment* could benefit from Lysol!

Checking the kitchen, Arlene opened the refrigerator. A half-consumed gallon container of milk, a carton of eggs, a pitcher, which probably contained juice or water. There was an open loaf of bread on the table and a small stack of unwashed dishes in the sink. Arlene could not help but notice the mousetrap on the floor, between the fridge and the stove. *She's got a little problem with mice,* she thought.

Checking done, both workers thanked Ms. Peters for her time and asked her to stay in touch. "Call me if you need anything or have any questions." Arlene said.

Downstairs, they looked at each other. "She's on something," Paulette said, "I think we need to get her screened like right away. Get PCS to screen her…you need to---"

A crowd that gathered near their car cut off her words. As they got closer they heard a din of sirens getting closer and closer. It was Arlene who screamed: *What the fuuuck???*

A set of legs were sticking up in the air, where the car's windshield was--or should have been!

****

Local Office Manager Marie Kovacs was in a dither.

She was under directive from her boss, Area Office Director Kathy Blasi to keep up the numbers in terms of MVRs, contacts, court reviews, etc. She knew that everyone was overworked, and cases backlogged, but there was so much more needed to be done.

Having met with two of her Case Work Supervisors, it was determined that the cases were taking too long of a time to be transferred from Intake to Permanency. And Adoption wasn't too far behind, either.

Kevin Beck was the Permanency CWS. He had four units in his tier, one of whom was Adolescent. Not one to make excuses--yet not one to give in to kowtowing or obsequiousness--Kevin explained that the Adolescent and one other unit took much time and paper, given the court reviews and all.

"Three workers got their heads handed to them by the judge," he said in the closed-door conference, "'Cause they were never given the opportunity to do the reviews, given the transferred cases, MVRs, and all."

"I understand that, Kevin," Marie said, not unsympathetically, "But now we've got the

Law Guardian and the DAG making sure that all the 'I's are dotted and all the 'T's crossed. And '1's don't become '4's. You know how it is."

Much back-and-forth bartering, negotiating, talking and planning, with half-hopes that the set plans would become fast goals.

It had not been a good month. An adolescent client had been placed in a foster home and in a short time, proceeded to set a fire. The entire house burned to the ground, the family losing everything. Marie was besieged with calls from the family's lawyers, her boss Kathy, and even the Commissioner.

Another client, a 14-year-old female, was discovered to be pregnant. The father was said to be her 22-year-old cousin, a young man with mental deficiencies.

In addition, a worker, transporting a client, was in a serious car accident--the worker's vehicle T-boned by a drunk driver. The worker suffered multiple cuts and contusions, but the young client was hospitalized with neck injuries.

Little doubt Marie was stressing, and when the boss takes shit, the shit flows downward. Now she had to deal with the slowness in transferred cases.

"I'm halfway up shit's creek with half a paddle," she reminded the "lieutenants" of the units, "So humor me, huh?"

The phone on Marie's desk rang and she picked it up. After a terse greeting, she listened briefly and felt herself stiffen. "What?" she said. A pause, then another "What?" followed by a third "What??" Another pause and she slammed the phone down in its cradle, her teeth clenched. *"SHIT!!"*

****

Parking his State vehicle, Nick went into the office. He checked in with his supervisor, Karen, and gave the details on Jeremy's court matter.

Karen Emory was a petite woman in her late forties with long brown hair and a cheery manner. She was a stand-up gal, in Nick and other workers' mindsets--that is to say, Karen will back you up when you know you are doing what you think is right. Even when it's not the "traditional" way, so to speak, you do what you gotta do.

"So as I understand it," she mused when

Nick finished speaking, "Jeremy was charged and fined five hundred dollars, right?"

"Yep," answered Nick, "And when we got there, before he even walked into the courtroom, he said he was gonna tell the judge to 'kiss his ass'."

"Oh, that would've gone over great," laughed Karen.

"And I told him," Nick continued on, "that the judge would kiss *his* ass with ninety days in jail."

"Hopefully, this'll teach him a lesson," Karen stated, but both knew that it would take more than a traffic matter for the kid to learn.

Back at his desk, Nick began the contact report for Jeremy's court matter. It was 2:45 in the afternoon and although he hadn't had lunch, Nick wasn't hungry. He finished the report and began working on a couple of school reports on another client when Bob approached him.

Bob Hendrick was a Family Service Specialist 1 in Nick's unit. He was the senior man in the unit, literally and figuratively. At sixty years old, Bob was about Nick's height yet about forty pounds heavier. The older man was at retirement age but Nick got the impression that he didn't want to retire. "Are you available to do this for me?" he asked Nick, handing him a TRF (Transport Request

Form).

Nick perused the form, noting the client name, address, pick-up, drop-off, etc. He saw that the date of the assignment was good--in other words, he was available. "Have Karen initial it and leave it in my box if I'm not here."

"Thank you, my good man." was the response from the older worker.

Finishing his reports, Nick pulled up Jeremy's case record on the computer. He had worked a few times with the young man and his mother, who had two other children. She was a single mom who took medication for depression and attended therapy sessions as well as a psychiatric evaluation.

Nick had been warned about the mom's emotional instability--in fact, one day she had come on to Nick very strongly, mouthing to him, "Let's get a motel room and have sex!" *That* prompted him to not transport or have any more contact with her, and he had told his supervisor this. The mom was placed in a mental facility for a time, the kids placed with an aunt.

Nick felt that if Jeremy had a positive male role model, a mentor, then maybe--just maybe--he could be put on the right path. But because of the cuts in State funding, very few services were available. Nick shook his head,

You can't save 'em all!

The phone on his desk rang and he picked it up. It was Karen. "Could you come to my office a minute?" He went in and Karen handed him the request form written by Bob. "Sit down a minute, will you please?" she asked. The door was closed and the supervisor informed him, "I got a complaint about you."

"Okay," Nick acknowledged, "What is it?"

"We both know it's bullshit," said Karen, "But Mr. Doakes called here railing and hollering. Said that you didn't put the bags in the van when you picked up the baby for her visit. Said you were rude and nasty."

Nick knew it all too well. Mr. Doakes was the paternal grandfather of Jamie, an 11-month-old infant girl who Nick transported and coordinated visits with her biological mom, who was in a drug rehab facility in South Jersey. Mr. Doakes seemed okay to Nick upon first meet, but it was noticed in a short time that the man was very bossy and dominant. Turned out that Mr. Doakes was a retired Army captain; he even gave orders to his wife!

"Now Karen, c'mon---" began Nick.

"I know, I know," Karen stated, "But he called Marie and boxed her ears about it. And Marie called me in to ask what's goin' on. I need you to write up a detailed report regarding your contacts with Mr. Doakes." Karen continued, "I need to know everything he said, word-for-word, how he acted, all that."

Always something, Nick thought as he returned to his desk. A couple of years before, he worked under a different LO Manager and Unit Supervisor. Nick and the supervisor, Fred, did not get along, and Nick had not had much more use for the then-LOM. Fred had claimed that there were "numerous complaints" about Nick; Nick, in turn, had asked to face his accusers, but Fred hemmed and hawed. Nick had further covered his ass by writing detailed contact reports containing date, time, place and nature of all occurrences--as well as names of parties involved.

He took it even further by making copies of his reports, forwarding each to his Unit Supervisor, Case Work Supervisor, Local Office Manager and even the Area Office Director! "Now," he said, staring Fred down in his office, "I've got *my* claims documented--where's *your* documented so-called 'complaints'?"

"I don't have nothin' documented…" Fred began.

"You don't have nothin' documented," Nick mimicked, "Then need I remind you of the

general fucking rule? If it ain't in writing, asshole, then *it doesn't exist!!* Got it??" Nick knew that he could get in trouble for speaking to a supervisor that way, but he didn't care. He was damn sick and tired of this guy trying to bully and intimidate people. Fred had actually driven two workers to tears. Eventually, he was transferred out and reassigned to another Local Office.

Nick had seen instances of heavy conflict in the LO. It was not always supervisor/worker; sometimes it was worker/worker. Two workers in a shouting match, cursing, name-calling. There was even a pushing-and-shoving match between workers, and a "I'll be seein' you out in the parking lot after work!" threat. In one case, two workers were suspended after an altercation that led to a near-brawl; the police were called and the combatants given an escort from the building.

Back to Doakes. Nick had a vivid memory of the happening between himself and the grandfather. Now the older man claimed that Nick had spoken to him in a threatening tone. Unbelievable. He wrote his detailed version of events, signed his name and submitted copies of same through the proper channels.

"Fanny asked if you could supervise her visit," said Karen when Nick handed her her copy of the report, "She has an emergent visit and would you sit in until she gets back?"

"When is it?"

"Tomorrow, visit's at 10." Karen handed him the request and Nick went to Fanny's desk for more information.

Assistant Family Service Worker Fanny Palumbo was a pert woman in her mid-thirties with an upbeat attitude and cheery personality. She gave Nick the required information and said she would try and be back from her detail as soon as she could. "Thanks Nick," she said, "It's just the visit, no transporting."

"Got it." he acknowledged. He went back to his desk, intending to finish off a couple more papers before ending his day. But then the phone on his desk rang again. "Nick," came the voice on the other end, "Need you for something, like now!"

****

"Fuck you, you slick-ass motherfucker! I ain't doin' *shit!* You can kiss my black ass 'fore I calm down!"

It was a client/parent transport, and AFSW Paul Zahorsky had brought a young mother and her infant son to JFK Medical Center for the child's appointment. The appointment had been set for 2 p.m. and Paul had arrived to the client home at 1:15, with plenty of travel time to the hospital.

The young mom was very confrontational and rude. She kept Paul waiting in the van for an interminably long time, and when she did finally load her son and herself into the vehicle, it was 2:15.

"You know that your appointment was for 2, right?" he asked when they pulled away from the residence.

"Don't matter," she said, "They'll see him anyway."

That's what you think!

They arrived to JFK at 2:50. Paul had pulled the State minivan in at the front door tom drop Mom and her son off, but she would not get out of the vehicle. "Go in there and see if they'll see him." she tried to order the worker.

Paul could hardly believe what he was hearing. "Wait a sec," he announced, "Hold the phone….you make yourself late, and now *you* try to tell *me* to 'go in and see if they'll see him'? I don't think so! You get in there and handle your son's affairs!"

The young parent went in, but not without a

few snide words. She came back out after a few minutes and said, "The motherfuckers won't see my son!" She was upset.

"Again," Paul stated, "Your appointment was for 2 o'clock; it's now 3. What'd you expect them to tell you?"

This resulted in a loud, angry tirade from the mother. She got so loud that her infant son began to cry. Paul waited it out, and then said calmly, "You done with your tantrum?"

No, motherfucker, I'm not done with my fuckin' tantrum! She proceeded to curse out the worker and scream at him with all the power in her lungs. This caused several passers-by to stop and look. Paul, having stepped out of the vehicle by this time, held up his hands, as if to say "Calm down", but the young woman misread this and made a move towards him.

Still screaming, she took an open hand and slapped the worker clear across his face. Paul in turn grabbed her by the wrists to avoid being struck further. Holding her, he realized that he was unable to reach for his cell phone to call 911.

Noticing the passers-by looking, and still struggling to avoid further assault, his eyes told the small crowd: *Call the police!* Instinct told him to let her loose, and Paul released his grip, hoping that maybe the mother would chill out. He could hear the baby crying uncontrollably, and he wished he could comfort the child. But not with Lady Godzilla on the rampage!

With that, she lunged at him again, her hands clenched into fists. It wasn't that he couldn't defend himself, but Paul could just see the headlines: *Child Services Worker Strikes Parent in Hospital Parking Lot.*

Hospital Security came to his rescue and a burly guard got between the young woman and Paul. Whipping out his cell phone, Paul called his supervisor and advised what had happened. The sup notified the primary worker, who called Paul back immediately. "What the hell's going on? What happened?" the worker asked worriedly.

Paul told the other worker.

"Is that girl out of her fucking *mind?* Jesus Christ….are you all right?" the worker was genuinely concerned.

"I'm fine," said Paul, "But the baby's going crazy here, cryin' and hollerin'."

Three Edison Township police cars pulled in, their roof lights flashing. The cops got out of their cruisers and Paul showed his Division credentials. Having hung up with the other worker, he explained to the officers what had happened, leading to the altercation. The officers took the young mother's name and information. A few minutes later, one of the officers approached Paul, "Don't know if you know this," the cop said, "But the young lady here's got a couple outstanding warrants. We're gonna have to take her in." Another officer was snapping handcuffs on the young mother's wrists and proceeded to place her in the back of one of the patrol cars.

"I'll need to notify my supervisor…tell what's happening." Paul said. The officer nodded and Paul punched in the number on his cell phone. He got the sup on the line and informed her of the latest.

"Is that girl outa her fuckin' mind?" the supervisor asked incredulously, "She's just a nasty, manipulative little *bitch!*" Paul cooled his heels while the sup vented, "She calls here every fucking day, demanding for us to do one thing or another for her and her baby…just too lazy to do shit for herself!"

And now, thought Paul, *the nasty, manipulative bitch is on her way to jail!*

"You still have the baby, right?" asked the supervisor.

Paul affirmed this. The sup put him on hold and in the interim, the patrol sergeant gave Paul information as to where the young woman was going. "She has $1,800 in outstanding warrants," said the sergeant, "We're taking her to County.

When the sup came back on the line, Paul conveyed this new information. "Bring the baby here," he was told, "I'm gonna have him looked over by the nurse."

Meanwhile, sitting in the back of the police car, her hands cuffed behind her back, the young mother stared out the window, tears rolling down her face. She remained mute during the ride to the county jail and upon arrival, as the officer was handing her to the deputy, she spoke: "I want charges against that worker drove me to the hospital!"

"Yeah?" one of the officers said, unconvinced, "What kinda charges?" he asked in a mimicking tone.

"He...tried to *rape me!*"

****

"So you were in an apartment checking on a family case, right?"

"That's right."

"And you say you heard a crashing noise while you were in the apartment, but didn't see anything?"

"Nobody bothered to look out the window," said Paulette, "We're here to service a family, not sight-see!"

Paulette Dahl was matching the detective's tone and demeanor, word for word. The State vehicle was surrounded by yellow crime scene tape. Patrol cars had blocked off the street, and a huge crowd had formed. From the workers' POV, just outside the taped perimeter, the car's windshield was totally shattered, its roof had a pronounced dent at the front where it met the windshield. A pool of blood and gray matter trickled along the hood.

Arlene, seeing disbelievingly, ran to a nearby tree and vomited. After an interminable time coughing and hacking, she managed--barely--to pull herself together. Paulette was ready to join her partner in the lunch discharge, but somehow kept it in.

Arlene had called it in to her supervisor while the police were sealing off the area. Both women knew that they were not leaving to go anywhere just now, until the Homicide detectives were finished with them.

"Wonder if Miss Peters is up there lookin' out her window at us." said Arlene.

"Wouldn't doubt it," answered Paulette, "And probably laughin' at us while gettin' snockered."

A car from the LO was sent to pick up the workers. Fanny, its driver, was nervous about being in the area. Parking two blocks away, she shut and locked the doors securely and walked quickly yet cautiously, her eyes sweeping her surroundings.

The AFSW saw her two colleagues and upon making contact, her eyes asked: *What the hell happened?* By this time, the body had been removed and placed in the Coroner's van. A tow truck appeared from seemingly nowhere to haul the State car to the police impound.

The detective returned. He questioned Paulette again, then Arlene. It was the same questions repeatedly, with the same answers repeatedly. "Is there anything else?" the detective asked.

"Like what?"

"Like whatever." the detective shot back.

"Look, we told you everything already, okay?" Arlene was irritated, "You got our names and information, you know where to reach us…we gave you everything we had…"

"All right," the detective said shortly, "Okay. Thanks. You can take off."

Without looking back, the three workers walked the two blocks to the car. They got in and, nary a word spoken, Fanny drove back to the office.

There, Arlene filled Bryan in on the MVR with Ms. Peters. When they discussed the body in the car, Bryan noticed a cloudy look over Paulette's eyes, as if she were in another world.

Both Bryan and Arlene noticed the faraway look. "Hey…Paulette…you all right?" asked Bryan.

Dismissively, Paulette answered, "Yeah…I'm good."

Bryan asked about the incident with the body in the car and upon mention, Paulette got up and left the office. Arlene went out after her. "Paulette," she called, "What's wrong? You sure you okay?"

"I'm *good!*" she snarled, "Just…go back and finish talkin' to Bryan, okay?" Paulette went down the hall and exited the building, Arlene staring after her.

"What was that all about?" Bryan asked. By this time, Case Work Supervisor Kevin Beck had joined him. Arlene shrugged silently.

A Division 21-10--Critical Incident Report-- had to be made out and submitted to Marie, and Arlene was prepared to do one, but it was without doubt: Something had spooked Paulette!

****

Nick had received the directive from Karen: He was to transport a male infant to temporary placement with the infant's maternal grandmother.

Paul was returning with the child. A nurse from CHU (Child Health Unit) was in the office to check the youngster's overall condition; there was probably no need for a doctor.

The LO had copies of the child's immunization records and most recent pediatric visits.

The grandmother, who lived about forty minutes away, had been phoned and notified of the situation. Obviously, she also knew of her daughter's incarceration. For this latest piece of news, she was hurt and upset, but she also knew of her daughter's wild temper tantrums.

"I keep tellin' her that she need to calm down," said the grandmother, a petite woman in her fifties, "And do she ever listen?" She shook her head. "I hate to say, but maybe her bein' lock up'll teach her somethin' a two 'bout her wild attitu'."

Nick heard about the incident involving Paul. He--Nick--knew the young woman and had seen some of her careless attitude, but not to the magnitude Paul had gone through. "You okay?" he asked when Paul got in.

Paul assured everyone that he was fine. He sat in a chair and recounted how the mom had swung on him. "Damn, I actually had to lock her wrists," he said, "to keep her from rearranging my face. She's small, but my God, that is one strong little girl!"

The baby, meanwhile, was being looked over by the nurse. Felicia Maynard, the CHU nurse on duty, was a full-figured woman with chestnut brown hair and a warm, girlish smile.

Paul had brought the infant in. After the incident, when he and the police had left the hospital, the baby had fallen asleep in his child seat during the ride to the LO. Now he was awake and crying again. Felicia was doing her best to soothe him, but she was fighting a losing battle. Another worker was in the room with the nurse--both the worker and the nurse had their hands full.

While Paul was finishing his story, Fanny joined them. She inputted the scene with the body in the car, the police, and the crime scene tape.

Paul and Nick both whistled. Fanny told them that the body had been removed from the car by the time she got there, "But you could see the hole in the windshield," she said, "A big fucking hole with blood and brain splatter!"

"Jesus Christ!" Nick shook his head. "And Arlene…Paulette…they all right?"

"Far as I know," said Fanny, "They both went into Bryan's office soon as they got in. A big pow-wow with Bryan, Kevin and Marie."

Others joined the three Assistant Family Service Workers as the stories recounted. "Man," said Kim Burkett, another AFSW, "So much shit happenin' in one day….like Murphy's Law. What's going on?"

They sat, stood, and leaned, all glancing at each other, looking for an answer. *What the hell is going on???*

****

Am I running the fucking Titanic *or what?!*
Local Office Manager Marie Kovacs was on her feet, yet stooped over her desk, palms flat against the desktop. She looked without seeing the mound of papers scattered across her desk as well as her Rolodex, calendar, and

SARs (Special Approval Requests) waiting to be approved.

Picking up the extension, she summoned Unit Supervisor Lisa Morales to her office. "Close the door and sit down," said Marie upon Lisa's arrival, "This is gonna take a few."

Lisa Morales was a short woman--five-foot-four inches--with shoulder-length brown hair. She was known for her outspokenness and her temper matched her height. The "human firecracker" of the LO, so she was known as when pushed.

"I just got a call from the County Sheriff's office," Marie filled her in, "There's been a complaint about Paul..." and the LOM told the Unit Supervisor about the young mother's claim.

Lisa didn't know whether to laugh or yell. She merely shook her head, "Now you know damn well that's not Paul," she said, "We've got stacks of problems concerning that little..."

"You know it, I know it, we all know it," said Marie, 'But she's filed a complaint. She's signed her name on it and everything."

Lisa sat in her chair, her mouth open as wide as the Lincoln Tunnel. "Oh, my God..."

Marie picked up the phone, dialed Paul's extension, and asked him to come to her office.

Paul took this latest news with mounting disbelief. He knew that he had shown professionalism and civility even when this parent was in his face. "She swung on me!" he said incredulously, "She got in my face, cursed me, called me all kinds of names…when I tried to calm her down, she actually took a swing at me!"

"I know, I know," Lisa said, trying to calm her worker down. She was just as upset as he was, but as a supervisor, she knew that she needed to show calm. She looked at Marie, "He will write up a detailed report as to what happened…"

"You're goddamn right I will!" Paul's voice reached a high volume, "I'll be damned if anyone's gonna accuse me of any shit…"

"We're not accusing you," Marie spoke directly, 'But we just need to go through the motions and cover our asses…"

"Cover *whose* asses?" Paul demanded, "Yours? Mine? Who do ya mean by *'our'???"*

Just as this question was asked, the phone on Marie's desk rang. She answered with every intention of telling the caller that she couldn't talk at the moment, but her statement was cut off by what she heard.

An adolescent client, recently placed in a

group home, was killed in a robbery attempt.

****

Gary Holmes was a wanderer.

His mother and maternal aunt had raised him in the Martin Luther King Housing Projects. His father, who had been in the Army, was killed in action in the Persian Gulf. Not that Gary had been close to his father--he had reenlisted while Gary was not much more than a toddler--but he had seen little of him when he was home.

The oldest of four children, Gary and his siblings were taken away from their mother some months ago, when it was discovered that the children were left to sleep in one dingy bed with a filthy mattress and covers. More to this was that the apartment in which the family lived--a one-bedroom--was never clean. The investigating worker noticed the smell of urine and feces emanating from the over-clogged toilet, but was spooked to the core when she saw two live mice gnawing on a piece of bread on the living room floor!

Gary and his brother were placed in an adolescent group home, while their younger siblings were placed in a resource home some distance away. No visits for a while, per the judge. Mom will just have to either straighten out her living arrangements, or find another place.

Gary, at age 16, was very street-educated and had many street resources. Much as the mentoring service contracted by the Division had tried to link him with positive outlets, he preferred to hang out with the "bad crowd". As a result, his school attendance was mediocre at best; he was on the fringes of expulsion when he decided to stop going to school.

With no other outlet, Gary obviously turned to the wrong people. He had seen the high-level dealers in their flashy Lexus and BMWs, rocking the fanciest clothes, the bling, and it intrigued him no end. He had gotten to know some of the street level dealers and a couple of suppliers, and was introduced to the world of selling.

But with this, Gary had also turned to using. A simple high turned into using more, which escalated to the point of his using what he was supposed to be selling, thus eating into his, and his supplier's, profits. This got him in trouble.

At first, his supplier had warned him about his habit; he had been told that the simplest mistakes could get him somewhere he did not want to end up!

His pockets bare, and desperate for money, Gary turned to pick pocketing, shoplifting, and muggings. He and a friend were leaning against a parked car one evening, making bullshit talk, each sizing up passers-by as they spoke in hushed volumes.

They nearly missed seeing the medium-sized man who double parked his car to walk into a nearby liquor store. The man went in to buy a six-pack and the boys noticed the wad of cash as he opened his wallet to pay for the beer.

Gary and his buddy exchanged glances-- they had found their "vic".

While one waited near the man's car, the other stood just outside the store. As the man walked out, he was followed--closely, but not too close-- while the other made his way from another direction. The attack was made just as the man reached the passenger side of his car. Gary wrapped his arm around the man's neck, placing him in a headlock, while the other kid punched him. "Give it up, motherfucker!" was the command.

They underestimated the man's agility. The

man threw Gary over his shoulder onto the hood of the car. As he did so, the other boy cold-cocked him with a left to his jaw. The man recovered quickly and pulled out his wallet--or, what was thought to be his wallet. It was black all right, like a wallet, but the black of a Glock 26 automatic pistol. Gary, not realizing what it was, attempted to leap onto his victim from the car's hood and as he did so, two shots were discharged from the "wallet".

The friend, realizing what was happening, threw his own hands skyward. "Okay, okay…" he hollered, "Don't shoot me…*please* don't shoot---"

"GET THE FUCK ON THE GROUND, ASSHOLE!! *FACE DOWN! NOW!!!*" the man screamed at him. The kid complied, placing his hands flat out while the man kept his gun pointed at his neck.

A small crowd was gathering. The man took a cell phone out from his jacket pocket and made a call. In a very short time, police cars were converging on the area, lights and sirens going. The cops jumped out of their cars with guns drawn.

Looking at Gary laying on the ground, the man noticed that his rounds had hit the boy in the upper and lower torso. Both rounds had exited his back. A pool of blood was forming and Gary was losing consciousness fast.

An ambulance raced up the street and screeched to a stop while the attendant in the passenger seat had the door open and was jumping out of its cab. The paramedics ran directly to Gary and began to administer aid. The other young man, now handcuffed, was being placed in the back of one of the police cars. He was by this time very pale and frightened. He took one last look at Gary as the officer sat him in the car--he knew it would be the last time he'd see his friend.

The intended victim came to the door of the car in which the boy was sitting. He wanted to ask a few questions. "Why did you do this?" he asked, "You know better than to do this….what got in your mind to pull such crazy shit?"

It was then that the man extracted his wallet--but not to give money. Just inside the fold was a badge!

Gary and his friend tried to rob someone. That "someone" turned out to be an off-duty cop!

****

Paulette Dahl was not "fine".

This latest event, she knew, put her in danger of going over the edge.

Having grown up in Irvington, Paulette had seen more than her share of dead bodies: gunshot victims, stab victims, auto accidents. More than her share of bloodshed.

Somehow, this was different, and only she knew it.

Paulette had been raised in a working-class family; her father was a bus driver for New Jersey Transit, while her mother was a cafeteria worker in the Newark public schools. By no means wealthy--but not poverty-stricken--Paulette felt that she had been raised "proper", given the standards of the community.

Having graduated high school with honors, she had enrolled into Rutgers, intending to major in Psychology with a minor in Law. One day while in college, three officers from the Newark Police had come to the school, conducting a Job Fair--the Newark P.D. was looking for good candidates to apply for and take the Civil Service exam for police officer.

Paulette did apply and take the exam. She scored significantly high.

Time passed. Paulette continued with her studies and all but forgot about the police exam. Letters and phone calls from the police department went unanswered. Given her current studies and potential career path (she wanted to become a therapist), Paulette had no interest in becoming a cop.

Graduating college with a Bachelor degree, Paulette had begun working as an intern at a youth shelter. Through an acquaintance, she was encouraged to apply for a job with the Division as a Family Service Specialist.

The years of schooling and career direction, however, were not without pain and heartache. During her second year in college, Paulette's father suffered a fatal heart attack at the young age of forty-three while working in the backyard. Mr. Dahl had been an active, hardworking man who supported his family and provided what he could.

Some eighteen months after her father's death, Paulette's mother was critically injured in an automobile accident. The impact left Mrs. Dahl with a brain injury and instability. Intense therapy followed, yet Mrs. Dahl was never the same as her old self.

Following all this about a year later, Paulette's brother was killed in a drive-by shooting. It was she who found him, his blood pouring onto her hands and clothing. Seventeen rounds were fired, four of whom entered his body. Wordlessly, the young man looked at his sister as he lay dying.

Helplessness and sorrow conveyed in his eyes before he could see or hear no more. The intended target--a local drug dealer--escaped with little more than a grazing.

And now, this latest happening. Seemed as though death and destruction followed her!

Forgetting Arlene, Bryan, anyone or anything in relation to the job, Paulette walked blankly to her car, climbed in, started the engine and drove away. Something was spooking her, and she knew it.

****

Back at his desk to write up the report on the incident in Edison, Paul sat fuming as he banged away on his computer keyboard.

A 12-year veteran with the Division, Paul had seen his own share of disgruntledness: disgruntled parents, disgruntled workers, disgruntled supervisors, disgruntled Law Guardians, DAGs, and even judges.

Nevertheless, he liked the job, despite the disgruntled this-that-and the other.

A former substitute history teacher, Paul had grown bored with teaching what he termed as "the same old stuff". he did love working with children, however. One day while at home surfing the Internet, he came across the site for the state Department of Personnel.

Deciding to take a closer look at the job listings posted therein, he noticed that the Division was seeking people to take the State Civil Service exam for Assistant Family Service Worker.

Intrigued, Paul applied, paid the filing fee, and several weeks later found himself in a high school classroom taking the examination.

More weeks passed, and he received a letter from Trenton: he had scored rather high and within a short time, Local Offices around the state began calling and asking him to come in for interviews.

Much to the consternation of his wife. Wendy Zahorsky had been raised differently, but understanding her husband's background and upbringing, married him despite. She never could understand the misfortunes of others.

"Why do you have to help people so much?" she asked him on more than one occasion. "Let them fend for themselves…it's not your fault that they have nothing!"

Paul did not share Wendy's thoughts. Being of Jewish background, he had learned much of the "Us versus Them" way of thinking;

within his high school and college years, he researched and studied about the Holocaust and Hitler's reign on the Jews. The movie *Schindler's List* had all but devastated him--he vowed to never watch it again. More frequently now, Paul wondered why Wendy, with her deep-rooted prejudices, had even married him. He explained to her more than once that by joining the Division, he felt that he could do a better job of helping families and have a better understanding of them, than he could teaching.

Now, a dozen years later, Paul was feeling the hard crustiness of cynicism weighing him down. He was trying very hard to not let the nagging feelings get at him, but they were there. He always believed that people were people, regardless of race, nationality, or ethnic background. However, he noticed more minority families--especially parents--harboring an attitude than white families. In this latest scenario, the mom was black. And she called him every dirty, rotten name she could think of. *Now,* he thought, *she's trying to jam me up on some bullshit charge? I don't think so, kiddo!*

Paul wrote his report, printed it out, signed his name along the bottom and made copies. He personally handed one to Lisa, another to Kevin, and the third to Marie. "If there's gonna be a big stink," he said to Lisa, "let me know right now! I'll bring in my Union rep *and* my lawyer!"

Lisa, seeing how upset he was, spoke soothingly, "Paul, calm down," she said, "It's all a bunch of bullshit and we both know it."

He looked at his boss with a hard glare.

"Look," she said, "Why don't you take some Comp time….go home, relax, get your mind off all this. You got anything for tomorrow?"

"I got the Miller visit," answered Paul, "Mom just called and confirmed. And I got some collaterals to finish."

"I'll get a trainee to do the visit," said Lisa, "And don't worry about the collaterals. Just go home. You've been through enough."

Back at his desk to retrieve his jacket, Paul briefly joined the other AFSWs, still in their huddle. Nick, Fanny, Kim, and another, Vanessa, looked at him with curious eyes.

"I'm takin' some Comp time." Paul told the group, "Need to get away from this place."

There was a small chorus of "Don't blame you"s, followed by Nick's "Get this job outa your mind. Try and take it easy, huh?"

"Talk to ya guys later." Paul said, and he was gone. The other workers looked at each other, shaking their heads. *Who the fuck would ever believe it?*

****

LO Manager Marie Kovacs was briefing three of her Case Work Supervisors and four of her Unit Supervisors on the Gary Holmes incident. She knew that she should have had all of her Sups--Unit and Case Work--in her office, but of those missing, two were in court, another was on vacation and the other on Maternity Leave.

Upon conveying the news, many of those in attendance stared at the floor or shook their heads in disbelief. Two gasped in shock.

The case itself had previously been assigned to Bob Hendrick, the senior worker in the Adolescent Unit. Yet in all the shuffle, it had been reassigned to another worker, this worker currently in court on another case. "Josie," Marie pointedly asked the worker's Unit Sup, "What was the status on Holmes before all the shit hit the fan?"

Josephine "Josie" Martindale was a tall woman, mid-forties-ish, with dark auburn hair and fair complexion. She had begun her career fresh out of Kean University, worked her way up the ranks from Trainee to Family Service Specialist 2 (FSS2); then Unit Supervisor, all in seventeen years--seventeen *long, hard years!* "Angie's last MVR was two weeks ago," said Josie, "Her contact sheet says Gary had popped in and out of the group home…staff said that he just came in and out at his own leisure, was marked AWOL a couple times. He never listened to anyone, didn't wanna follow rules, etc."

"Shit!" they both thought aloud, "Angie still hasn't been notified yet!" Angie was the assigned worker.

"You need to get her on the phone," Marie ordered, "I know she's in court, but we need to get her in here--fast!" Josie excused herself to go make the call.

Turning to Bryan, Marie asked detailed questions about the incident involving Arlene and Paulette. The sup explained the happenings, adding in the faraway look on Paulette's face. "She just looked worse and worse," said Bryan, "Arlene and I both asked her if she was all right. She just nodded and said not a word. Arlene went out to look for her, even went out to the parking lot. Her car was gone."

An audible sigh from Marie. "Call her?"

"She's not answering. Goes straight to voice mail."

The LO boss sat back in her chair, thinking. One of the Case Work Supervisors, Annette Martinez, chimed in, "So now we have a dead client, two workers who witnessed another dead body in the windshield of their car, one of those workers zoned out…"

"…and yet another worker accused of rape." Marie finished.

"Marie," piped up Lisa, her fuse lit, "Now you know damn well---"

"Yes, yes, I *know!*" the LOM said testily, holding up a hand, "But you know we still gotta go through the motions."

"I'd like to go through that little bitch's motions!" Lisa could barely hold her temper.

"Lisa, take it down!" said Marie, "That whole thing involving Paul is on the back burner just now. I've got his report."

The door opened and Josie walked back in, with Angie in tow. Angie Franconero was an olive-skinned woman in her late-twenties, medium height, with shoulder-length jet black hair and brown eyes. She came to the Division right out of the U.S. Army, in which she had been a Staff Sergeant. She had served a brief tour in the Persian Gulf and upon her return home, finalized her DD-214s and got out.

Angie had experienced plenty of fear overseas. But now it seemed some fear had returned--for her colleagues and bosses could read it in her eyes. *What the hell is going on?* she wanted to yell, but kept her composure.

"I take it that Josie's told you?" inquired Marie.

"She told me some," Angie glanced in her Sup's direction, "But let me have it." She steeled herself for the news.

Marie told her. The worker stood staring at the LOM while the other spoke, and then slowly lowered her head. As the news sunk in, tears filled the worker's eyes, rolled down her face and dropped onto the floor; the tears black with mascara. "My God," she said repeatedly, not knowing what else to say.

"I understand that your last MVR was two weeks ago." Marie spoke.

Angie nodded slightly, then said, "Him and his brother…the group home staff said Gary was 'in and out all the time'…not tellin' anybody where he was goin', what he was doin'…

"When I last seen him he just said a quick 'Hi'. When I asked him how he was doing, he said he was okay. I asked him directly if he was still going to school and he said yes…I should have just went ahead and gotten his school record…"

"School or no, he might've still got in trouble," asserted Josie, "From what I understand, he was in deep with some drug dealers."

"But to rob someone--an off-duty cop at

that," spoke Marie, "*That's* gonna weigh heavy. Imagine the news coverage. And once they find out he had an open case…"

"I just got the case a little more than two weeks ago," Angie said in defense, "Surely you couldn't expect I should know *everything,* up to and including the times of day this kid *went to the bathroom…*"

"Nobody's blaming you, Angie," said Josie, shooting a glance at Marie, "Just saying that a tragedy has occurred, involving one of our clients---"

"You mean one of *my* clients!" Angie looked at her, faded black streaks on her face, "My client, killed on what was supposed to be my watch!" Her voice was rising as she spoke, anger flashed in her eyes.

"Okay, okay, calm down," Marie spoke soothingly, "Take a deep breath. We all know now what went down. The next step is to make sure all the paper is done to cover our asses. Angie, could you pull up all your 26-52s on the Holmes? I'm gonna need everything you've got, coupled with everything Bob did when he had the case."

"Will do." Angie nodded slightly.

Turning to CWS Annette Martinez, Marie said, "You need to get all of Bob's stuff as well. Get him down here, both of you go through everything. And I mean *everything* on that family and bring it all straight to me. Pronto!"

Angie headed for the door. "Angie," called Marie.

"What?" she said, turning to look at the boss. She was still fuming.

"Take it easy," said Marie, "This could've happened to anybody."

"But it didn't happen to just *anybody,* did it?" she replied sharply. With that, she was gone to wash her face and pull herself together.

Everyone else in the room sat, or stood, looking at each other.

****

A Division 26-52 is a Client Contact Form, written out on *NJ SPIRIT*, the database for the Division. Within the Form is written all varieties of client and family contact--be it an MVR (Minimum Visitation Requirement); client/parent transports; parent/family visitations--whether at home or in the office; or even court reviews, court appointments, medical or other appointments. Telephone contacts are also recorded within.

The Form is by and large done by a worker, be it an AFSW or FSS; it covers date, time, place, and nature of contact; case name; name(s) of party or parties contacted; and all happenings within. This in turn is forwarded to the worker's Unit Supervisor for approval. In extraordinary circumstances, it may also be forwarded to the Case Work Supervisor (to whom the Unit Sup reports), and/or the Local Office Manager. In even rarer cases to the Area Office Director.

Each LO is headed by a Manager. This LO Manager commands the office and oversees all staff within. The LOM reports to the Area Office Director; this person will oversee operations in numerous LOs, all within neighboring counties.

Arlene found herself doing a Form. Per Bryan, her 26-52 needed to be printed out and signed; a copy given to all of her superiors-- up to and even including Marie.

As a FSS Trainee, Arlene knew that her part was vital. Though busy writing, her mind kept wandering back to Paulette.

Arlene Rollins was brought up "the hard way". Born and raised in Newark, she had been involved with street gangs in her youth. Her father, who deserted his family ("He was nothin' but a sperm donor!" she would later claim) was currently serving 25-to-life in a South Jersey correctional facility for armed robbery and drug possession. Arlene's mother worked two jobs to support her family, but after losing one job for habitual lateness, she fell behind on her rent and the family was evicted from their small apartment.

Arlene was thirteen when this happened. At the shelter, she met and befriended several other kids. She didn't realize it at the time, but she was "recruited" into a gang; this was done by being "jumped" by a group of other young teens and beaten. Having no other choice, Arlene knew that she had to fight back.

And fight she did. Soon, she discovered, her clique had advanced from using fists to using knives, and Arlene saw several kids stabbed-- not just from hers, but from other gangs. Shortly thereafter, a couple of her "friends" had obtained guns. Random shootings began to happen, and on one occasion, Arlene was with a small group of others on a drive-by. Luckily (for her), she had never been caught, but a number of her friends were not so lucky and sent away to stir.

Arlene's mentoring came in the form of a local church pastor. This pastor was himself a former street gang member and while serving time in prison, had turned to books for solace-

-the most notable book he read in prison: the Holy Bible.

Arlene was at first indifferent to the mentoring. But the pastor relented patiently, for he saw something in the young lady's eyes that conveyed innocence. After some time had passed, Arlene did warm up and asked questions--one or two, then more. Slowly she found herself turning from the word of the Gang banger to the word of God.

Divine Intervention? Wisdom? Who knows? But the truth of the matter is that Arlene eventually began attending school again on a daily basis. Her grades improved and graduated high school, she signed up for courses at NJIT. It was also at this time that Arlene began some youth mentoring of her own with hardcore gang members, talking to these street-hardened kids in their own language, utilizing her ex-gang member skills.

Discovering that she loved working with children, Arlene applied for and took the Civil Service exam to become a Family Service Specialist.

And now here she was, a FSS Trainee, working in the field with families in similar situations to those of her own past experiences.

Prior to her appointment to the Division, she had met Paulette when the other was a Trainee herself, and Arlene was a private sector mentor. Now, here they were, working together. Although they hadn't known each other strongly, it was almost like Homecoming when Arlene was welcomed to the LO. She and Paulette spoke about past experiences, engaged in some shop talk and enjoyed each other's company. Arlene had looked to Paulette to take her under her wing and show her the ropes.

And the Trainee did learn much about the job from her new mentor. But now, Arlene knew in her gut, her mentor was in trouble. A ton of trouble!

****

Francesca DiCiccio had fallen on tough times.

She was a single mom of two who lived on her late husband's benefits.

Unemployed, and no other visible means of income, Francesca--know to her friends as Fran--had taken various off-the-books jobs. She did maintenance work at a local deli, babysat some of her neighbors' children, and had done some crossing guard duties.

Fran was also a stern mom with a harsh temper. On more than one occasion, she was observed disciplining her children. What was not observed--and few people knew--was that Fran also had a cocaine addiction.

She made the mistake one coke-filled afternoon of locking one of her children out of the house. The youngster, a nine-year-old boy, was accused of purposely returning home late from school. The weather was cold and overcast, with temperatures in the upper-20s, and the boy was left outside with his school backpack, shivering and crying.

A passer-by, who knew the boy slightly, had noticed the youngster's plight. This person knocked on the front door to try to intervene, but to no avail. "He knows why he's out there," came the shout from within, "I want he should learn his lesson about comin' home late!"

The police were called and the boy, so cold now that his fingers were turning blue, was placed in the police car to warm up while the officers knocked on Fran's door and ordered her to open up.

The door was opened and the officers entered. On a coffee table they found remnants of fine white powder and a folded matchbook. Mrs. DiCiccio had a glazed, faraway look about her and was unsteady. "You got no fuckin' right ta order me ta open my door an' force your way inta *my* house!" she shouted at the officers. "Who the *fuck* ya think youse are?" she continued to holler.

One officer turned and got directly into the mom's face, "You left a child outside in the cold," he asserted harshly, "A nine-year-old child! In *this* weather? Are you fucking *brain-dead* or something?"

The second child, a seven-year-old girl, was located in a bedroom. Another officer had taken her by the hand and gently led her out to where the mother and the first officer were exchanging words. By this time, a sergeant had arrived to the home, and the Division was notified. "We're taking the kids with us," said one of the officers, "They're gonna be turned over to the Division…probably not coming back here."

Another officer was now handcuffing Fran, "And you're under arrest for possession," this second cop said to her, "You're going to jail for that and child endangerment!" The children by now had begun to cry.

"Fuck it," said Mrs. DiCiccio, "I'll be outa jail before the fuckin' paperwork's done…and just wait 'til I get that fuckin' worker's name who takes my kids! I got somethin' for *that* bitch!"

What even fewer people knew about Fran DiCiccio was that she was the niece of Dominick "Heavy Legs" Valenza, *sotto capo,* or "underboss", of one of New Jersey's largest Mafia Families!

****

Nick, having finished his report, signed out for the day. He had an early client pick-up the next morning and had secured a child seat for the youngster. He got into his Division-issued minivan and started home.

Turning up the radio as he drove, he relaxed as the minivan rolled along the highway. Nick lived by a certain "code of ethics", so to speak--one being that he would never take the job home at night. The job *vehicle,* on occasion, but never the job itself.

Arriving home some forty-five minutes later, he walked in and was greeted by Amy, his live-in girlfriend.

Amy Paladino was a slightly curvy woman in her early-forties of above-average height-- five feet ten--with jet-black hair and hazel eyes. A former hospital triage nurse, she had changed careers and now worked as a bank officer. "How was your day?" she asked as they kissed.

"Okay, I guess," he answered, "The usual bullshit." He knew that the day was more than "the usual bullshit". In fact, it was rather extraordinary! But just now, he didn't want to go into detail. Maybe later, but not now. Nick looked at Amy and she returned his eye contact. "What's wrong?" she asked, some alarm in her voice.

There was nothing wrong, he assured her. But looking at her, he couldn't help but to think of her sweetness, her tenderness.

They had met online, five years ago. Nick had been with the Division a year; Amy lived in Delaware and had just left her job at a hospital due to burnout. She was working as a teller at a local bank.

Nick and Amy spoke every day. Online chats and e-mails soon became daily phone calls, sometimes two to three calls per day. As they spoke, they got to know each other better.

Taking a vacation day from work, Nick drove to Delaware to meet Amy, face-to-face. Pictures had been exchanged long prior to the trip and each knew what the other looked like.

Amy lived with her mother; her father had

passed away nearly ten years ago. The elder woman was sweet, yet Nick noted caution in her eyes. "You be good to my daughter!" she warned with a smile, but Nick knew that behind that smile was a stern, serious warning.

Nick and Amy enjoyed that weekend immensely. Trips to the beach, shopping, romantic meals and--in between--a good deal of time spent in bed! Neither had ever been married, nor there were any children. Their time was their time.

The Sunday of that weekend was a letdown for both. Walking Nick to his car, Amy took his face in her hands and they kissed passionately.

As he drove away, heading toward the Turnpike, Nick found himself wiping the moistness from his eyes. He called her upon his return home, as she had made him promise to. The phone conversation lasted the better part of two hours.

After several months of subsequent trips to Delaware--and Amy's trips to Jersey as well-- Nick asked Amy to move in with him. Amy at first was hesitant, for she had been born and raised in Delaware and did not want to leave her mom. Nick assured her that she could see her mom anytime she wanted and without any interference.

He kept his word. Amy packed her belongings, and with a U-Haul rented, paid for, and driven by Nick, made the big move to the Garden State.

The first week in the new home was uneasy for Amy, despite her boyfriend's efforts to make the transition a smooth one. Amy missed her mom, her friends, her family and surroundings. Nick understood this, and treaded lightly. "You can always go back," he told her, "I will never come between you and your family." She appreciated his gesture more than he realized.

Time passed, and the homesickness, while not going away completely, waned. Amy got a job at a bank as an account officer. She liked her job, and did not miss the craziness and ugliness of hospital work. Some weeks later, after a much healthier account balance, Amy and Nick found themselves taking trips to Delaware to see her family. These excursions became weekend activities as they both worked Monday through Friday with weekends off.

Other times they went to the Shore, flea markets, festivals, even taking the bus into New York City to go to Central Park, Rockefeller Center, and other places. Amy loved Nick and developed a deeper fondness for him than he knew.

Now, in the present time, Nick was looking at her. Before he realized what he was doing, he was slowly undressing her with his eyes. Amy was physically impossible to resist. He just wanted to…

"Dinner's gonna be ready in about ten minutes," she said, breaking his thoughts. "Better get cleaned up." she added, smiling at him. He could swear that she also winked at him. *She knew what I was thinking!*

"Uh," he stammered, "Yeah, right." He had already taken his jacket off, laid his keys and cell phone on the table upon entrance. Now it was off to the bathroom for a quick shower.

Over dinner, Nick and Amy spoke. Nick hardly ever discussed the job in detail, but he couldn't get Paul out of his mind. Nor the youngster who had been killed in the robbery attempt. He explained, leaving out the kid's name. *It'll probably be on the news anyway,* he thought. It always makes news when someone is killed by a cop--crime or no crime. Amy sat listening, obviously sympathetic. "Poor kid," she said.

"You mean 'Poor *Paul*'." corrected Nick. "That kid tried to take off the wrong person and paid for it. Of all people….him and his friend messed with the wrong guy!"

Amy said nothing. Nick had no sympathy for the young punk--he got what he was asking for! Paul, on the other hand…he'd do whatever he could for his colleague. *He's* the one who got the bum rap.

After dinner, they settled down for the evening. Amy, feeling affectionate, leaned close to her man while watching television; Nick, teasing, gave his lady small playful pecks across her face, eventually landing onto her lips. After a time, each looked into the other's eyes and the unspoken word was conveyed.

Within seconds, the TV was off, the phones muted, and the pair was in their bedroom.

Amy Paladino was a voracious lover who gave as well as took. She and Nick made passionate love and upon climax, she screamed with relief and true satisfaction of fulfillment.

Shortly afterward, their bodies spent and feeling much better, small talk was made. It was at this time that Amy turned to Nick and said: *I'm late for my period…*

****

Paulette Dahl drove like a blind person.

Ignoring a stop sign, she nearly collided with another car at an intersection, miraculously avoided hitting a pedestrian crossing the street, and had a half-dozen people--pedestrians and other drivers alike-- yelling and cursing at her in her wake.

She stopped at a house in a run-down area, went inside and spoke with someone. After making a second stop at a liquor store, she made her way home, still driving like a maniac.

Her mom was in the downstairs bedroom. Paulette could hear the TV playing and doubtless, the elder Dahl was either watching a boring talk show, or nodding in her chair.

Paulette threw her keys and handbag onto a table and went upstairs. The second level of the house contained her own bedroom as well as that of her late brother and a second bathroom. It was to the former in which she went.

Two alcohol-dulled hours later, Paulette emerged. Her eyes were red-rimmed and her equilibrium left something to be desired. Descending the stairs, she stumbled badly and nearly fell. Despite the unsteadiness, she knew to check in on her mom. As Paulette had figured, her mom was settled in her wheelchair, her head against her plus-sized chest.

Paulette proceeded into the kitchen. She went to the refrigerator at first, then to the stove. Looking back toward the kitchen door, she did some fumbling with her hands, and then sat at the small table situated in the middle of the kitchen. Sitting, she closed her eyes and allowed her mind to go totally blank.

This was at 5:14 p.m. Three hours later, a massive explosion shattered the Dahl home, claiming the lives of two women.

****

Bob Hendrick was working SPRU (SPecial Response Unit). It was he who took the call on the DiCiccio removal.

With assistance from Fanny Palumbo, Bob had picked up Mrs. DiCiccio's children from the police station. While Bob--an old-timer of the Division, 31 years to be more exact--was completing the emergent DODD and speaking with the officers, Fanny was with the children, making every attempt to comfort them. The children, while frightened, were rather calm and somewhat receptive to the worker.

Bob liked and respected Fanny's open, caring attitude. Single and childless herself, Fanny possessed a natural childlike manner and knew how to communicate with children on their own level without condescension.

As Fanny was leading the youngsters toward the door leading out of the station, Mrs. DiCiccio, still handcuffed, was being led from the booking desk to a holding cell; it was during such that she got a glimpse of the Division worker with her children. In that brief look, Fanny could see the blood in the mother's eyes.

Your ass is mine, bitch! MINE!!!

In most, if not all cases, threats from parents--verbal or otherwise--are taken with a grain of salt. Parents in general despise child protective service workers--especially those who have had their children taken away! Not giving it a second thought, Fanny loaded the children into the State vehicle. Bob soon emerged from the station with a sheaf of papers and slid into the front passenger seat. The children had to be taken to a local hospital to be looked over by a doctor, then to a temporary resource home.

Fanny, at the wheel, remained her caring

self, but became less cheery as time went on.

"What's wrong?" Bob asked quietly at one point.

"Nothing," was the response. But something, she felt, was. Something, she felt in her gut, about Mrs. DiCiccio. There was something about that *look…*

****

Holy Jesus, Mary and Joseph!

Bryan Taylor got the call at his home. It was 12:45 at night and he was in bed. His wife, Yolanda, took the call and shook him awake. He took the receiver wondering: *Who the hell is calling at this time of night?*

"You're gonna hear it on the news," Marie Kovacs spoke matter-of-factly, her voice low and somber, "But let me break it to you…"

And it was upon hearing about Paulette that Bryan shouted his words. He had no idea what else to say. That one of his workers and her mother were killed in a house explosion made him nearly jump out of his skin.

When he hung up, he conveyed the news to his wife, who had only heard his end of the conversation. Yolanda was quite sympathetic and comforted him as best she could. He could now remember the last time he saw Paulette, that faraway, detached look. Bryan did not sleep for the remainder of that night!

Arlene Rollins had learned of the tragedy on the TV. She was watching *American Idol* when Fox 5 broke in with a news bulletin: *A house explosion, killing two people and injuring three others...*

The Fox 5 reporter on the scene gave the address and Arlene, holding a glass in her hand, dropped it upon hearing. The glass crashed to the floor. "Oh, my GOD!" she said repeatedly. Collapsing on her couch, she sobbed openly and wanted to ignore the phone when it rang.

Apparently, the news had spread like a prairie fire. An acquaintance of both Arlene and Paulette had called, followed by a fellow worker, then Marie and CWS Kevin Beck. Her boyfriend had also called, and he, not knowing what had happened, was told. Arlene assured him and everyone else with whom she spoke that she was fine. Needless to say, it was going to be one sleepless night.

Nick Donovan had left his home at 6:30 a.m. for his client pick-up. The youngster, a 4-year-old, was being transported to his day care facility from a resource home.

During the transport, he thought of Amy, and the possibility of their becoming parents. Until now, he had never considered having children. That he might become a dad tickled him in a way. *My own son or daughter,* he thought, *a child…looking up to me, calling me "Dad".*

He looked in the rear-view mirror at the young client in the car seat, imagining the youngster as his own, calling him "Dad". He couldn't help but smile at the thought as he brought the child in to his day care and the staff therein.

After dropping off the young man, Nick made a quick stop for coffee at a Dunkin' Donuts and then headed to the office. Coffee in hand, he walked in and immediately noticed the quiet, somber attitude among his colleagues.

Nick's own face clouded as he went to his desk, "What's goin' on?" he asked, knowing something had to be *not* good.

"You didn't hear?" asked Kim.

"Hear what?"

"Paulette and her mom were killed last night. Their house blew up."

"*WHAT??!!*" shouted Nick.

"They're sayin' it was a gas explosion…gas leak…no warning…just…went up." Kim shook her head.

"You friggin' kiddin' me???" Nick said, not believing.

"Couple workers ran outa here crying," Kim went on, "Marie's got all the sups and case work sups in a closed door…Kathy's in there, too."

"Kathy Blasi?" Nick asked, "Area Director?"

"Yep."

Nick sat in his chair, looking without seeing, "Holy shit!" he muttered, "I figured that that body in the car kinda spooked her. Fanny had said so. But now for this to happen to her…"

"That ain't all, now that you mention Fanny," Kim spoke again.

Nick looked at his coworker, his eyes saying, *What else now?*

"Fanny got a call from some dude, sayin' she was gonna get both of her legs broken. Apparently, she messed with the wrong people."

"How so?" asked Nick.

"Her and Bob did a DODD yesterday. Two kids. Anyway, mom got bailed outa jail either late last night, early this mornin'. She found out the workers' names took her kids. Had somebody call up and ask to speak to Fanny. Fanny took the call and the dude tells her what's gonna be done to her, she don't give mom her kids back, pronto!"

"Lot of parents make threats and stuff," said Nick dismissively, "Happens all the time."

"Right," said Kim, "But in this case, guess who the mom's related to?" And she told him.

"Holy *shit!*" Nick said with gravity. *Who the hell would believe this? Who WOULD believe it?* he thought. "Where's Fanny now?" he asked, "Is she all right?"

"I think she's in Liz' office," Kim answered. "She's still a little shaky." Liz was a Case Work Supervisor.

Nick further learned that the Human Services Police, as well as the local and State Police, were called in on the matter. "They might even call the FBI in on it," he was told.

Nick and the others in his unit were called in to a closed-door conference with Karen. Obviously, the tone of the meeting was maudlin, the air heavy. Karen spoke of the tragedy involving Paulette; a sympathy card will be going around the office with donations. With all her immediate family now gone, Paulette was survived by a maternal aunt. It would be to she that all donations and flowers will be sent.

"Of course, no funeral arrangements made just yet." said Karen.

Nick did not want to bring up the subject involving Fanny, but it was briefly discussed. "There may be a little more police presence in the next few days," Karen announced to the unit, "But just cooperate, go about your business as usual."

After the meeting, Nick returned to his desk. His cell phone rang and he saw it was Amy. They spoke for a few minutes and it dawned on him: *She doesn't know what's happening here!* He decided against telling her--at least over the phone. He did tell her that there had been some goings-on since he got to work that morning, but did not go into detail. "I'll tell you when I get home." he assured her. From his tone, Amy knew that it was too deep to get into just then. They blew their over-the-phone kisses and Nick broke the connection.

Throwing himself into his work, Nick tried to forget the surroundings and thoughts plaguing him: his concerns about Paul, Fanny, Amy's possible pregnancy…and now Paulette's death.

****

"She actually had somebody call and *threaten* me!"

Fanny was sitting in a chair in Case Work Supervisor Liz Jackson-Harper's office. Outwardly, she was calm. Her trembling had stopped for the most part and her voice even, but inside she was anything but.

Sipping water from a Styrofoam cup, she sat deep in thought. About her safety. About the job. About everything.

Elizabeth Jackson-Harper (her married name hyphenated) was a full-figured black woman in her early-fifties. She was a 24-year veteran of the Division who began her career as a Trainee. Another who worked her way up the ranks. She was less than a year away from retirement and had seen it all in her years on the job.

Now she was closely watching her AFSW, who felt--if not looked--vulnerable. "Is there someone we can call?" she asked.

Fanny, still in thought, shook her head, "I don't wanna get anybody else involved," she asserted, "This is my problem, guess I need to deal with---"

"*Our* problem!" corrected Liz, cutting the

other off, "We got the police involved as you know already…do you need someone to take you home?"

"Nah," said Fanny, "I can handle getting home on my own. I'm a grown woman."

"I *know* you're a grown woman!" Liz said incredulously, "I never meant it like it sounded."

"Thanks anyway,"

They sat in silence for another few seconds, then Fanny spoke again, "I was wondering…why am I the one being threatened? I was there with Bob, didn't that woman see him also?"

"Hate to say it," answered Liz, "but if you look at Bob, he kinda looks like a cop. Got the build and appearance."

"Even with the shirt and tie?"

"Shirt and tie, she musta figured him for a detective," Liz replied, "That's how detectives dress, don't'cha know."

She's got a point, thought Fanny.

"Is there anybody at home?" asked Liz.

"My brother's in and out all the time." answered Fanny.

"Wait," Liz spoke up again, "Didn't you say your brother was…a cop or somethin'?"

"Fireman," said Fanny, "But I just told you, I'm not getting anyone else involved---"

"Okay, okay, calm down," Liz held up a

hand, "I'm not askin' you to get nobody else involved. Especially your own family."

"Where's Mrs. DiCiccio now?" Fanny asked, to change the subject.

"Well, you know she got bailed out, right?" Liz said, "At this point, she's probably back home."

Or, thought Fanny, *she could be lurking somewhere outside, waiting for me.*

"Maybe you could go someplace?" Liz offered, "Your parents' house or something?"

"My folks live in Pennsylvania," Fanny answered, "I'm not gonna impose on 'em or bother 'em---"

"But they *are* your parents!" emphasized Liz, "And I'm sure they do love you will be glad to have you there."

The usually-perky AFSW considered this. The CWS sitting behind the desk did have a point. It had been a while since she had seen her mom and dad. Regular phone conversations aside, they had not actually been together in some time. Maybe it *was* time to pay a visit: take some time off, relax, and spend time with family...

"Not to be so personal," Liz piped up, "but is there someone you're close with---"

"I don't have a boyfriend, if that's what you're getting at." said Fanny. *No steady boyfriend,* she thought, *but I thought I did.*

The thought stemmed from a semi-relationship she had had a couple years back. She had met a man at a media venue who worked as a trade columnist. They became friends and realized that they had had much in common.

The down side: the man was married. Fanny had met and befriended his wife, and the two women got along just fine, even laughing and joking with each other.

However, the marriage was doomed, and Fanny knew this. After a time, she fell in love with this man, and the two began a discreet romance. Estranged from his wife, the man began to spend more time with his new lover.

While no virgin, Fanny had had little sexual experience. It was this man with whom she enjoyed the sex more and more. Seemed that she couldn't see him without wanting to go to bed with him!

Nevertheless, as fate would have it, the man returned to his wife. On more than one occasion during their relationship, Fanny pleaded with him to leave his wife and be with her. The man considered it seriously, but in the end decided against it.

It just was not meant to be.

Broken hearted and hurt, Fanny never saw or spoke to him again.

"…did you hear what I said?" Liz' voice cut

in, breaking Fanny's thoughts.

The other shook her head, as if to clear it. "Huh? What?" She looked at Liz now.

"I said, you might wanna call your mom, tell her you comin' for a few days!" the older woman repeated.

"Uh, yeah…okay." was the reply.

"You already know what to do," said Liz, "Fill out the paperwork and bring it to me. I'll sign it."

Back at her desk, Fanny filled out the Division 8-82 (Leave Request Form) and noticing her accrued Compensation time--she had well over 80 hours, roughly equivalent to 12 days--marked five days as Comp, the other five as Vacation. Taking the completed form back to Liz, the other scratched her signature, and upon doing so looked up at Fanny and said, "I'm unofficially givin' you today off as well."

Fanny began to protest, "But I've got---"

"A-ta-ta-ta-ah-ah-uh-uh-UH, I don' wanna hear it!" the CWS protested back, "I'll get somebody to cover whatever you got scheduled. Now I'm orderin' you: *Get on outa here!* Go! Enjoy your time off!"

No sense in fighting a Case Work Supervisor. More to the point: *No sense in fighting Liz Jackson-Harper!* "Okay, okay," Fanny said, smiling, her hands up in surrender, "I'm outa here. See ya."

"Hey, enjoy your time off, and don't you worry about nothin', okay?" Liz said in parting.

Fanny got her bag from her desk, shut her computer down, and walked out to her car. She started the engine and began driving in the direction of her home. About five minutes into the drive, her car began to stall and hesitate. *Guess I need a tune-up,* she thought at first, but as the car really began to act up, it backfired from its exhaust and then finally, with little warning, the engine died.

Having the common sense to coast it to the shoulder, Fanny got out and opened the car's hood. Knowing very little if anything about the mechanics of a car, she had no idea what to look for.

Drawing her cell phone, she began to punch in a number. She hadn't finished dialing when she noticed a car pull sharply onto the shoulder just ahead, then back up toward hers. The phone had just begun to ring on the other end when Fanny recognized the face of the occupant now exiting the vehicle--the face of Mrs. Francesca DiCiccio!

****

FSS Trainee Angie Franconero was printing out her client contact reports regarding the Holmes case. Comparing her notes with those of Bob Hendrick, the previous case worker thereon, both presented their written findings to Marie. As they sat waiting while she pored over several reports, Bob noticed the changes with the LO boss. There were more wisps of gray in her brown shoulder-length hair, which was usually tied in a ponytail; the crow's feet at the corners of her eyes were deeper; her brown eyes, once bright and sparkly, were now dark and tired-looking.

Marie had been the Local Office Manager for five years. She held a Master's degree in Social Work and a Teaching degree. She had started her career some twenty years ago as a grade-school teacher, had risen to the Administrative level and eventually became an assistant principal--all the while attending school and earning her degree. Handpicked by Area Office Director Kathy Blasi, with the blessings of the Commissioner, Marie replaced the old LOM, who retired after 31 years with the Division.

Bob Hendrick, considered a "lifer", for he himself was a veteran of old, had seen LOMs come and go in the several offices out of which he worked during his long career.

And Marie, seated at her desk, was deciphering the various papers set before her. "So…" she spoke now, "From what I gather, Gary was a chronic runaway…"

Bob was the first to respond, "Everywhere he was placed, he ran away from. Even when he was home, he wandered the streets. No telling where or what he was up to when he was in that group home…"

"His school record was, at best, mediocre." Marie spoke again, "Where the hell does a 16-year-old go during the day, when he's supposed to be in school?" It was a rhetorical question.

"Angie, your last MVR," Marie addressed, "You said you saw him but briefly, yes?"

The other worker affirmed.

"And the staff there told you that he was 'in and out all the time', is that right?"

"Correct."

Marie tossed the papers down onto the desk and sat back in her chair. "Well," she sighed, "He's sixteen--or he was sixteen. What were we supposed to do? Hog-tie him? I feel bad about it, but the only thing we can really do is comfort his mom and brother."

"They could sue, can't they?" asked Angie, "I mean, his mother could---"

"She could sue," Marie cut her off, "but would she actually collect? Probably not. Look, yeah, the family was--is--Division-involved, but *we* tried our part in implementing positives for him; *he* decided to ditch school, roam the streets and deal drugs.

"Look, I don't mean to sound so harsh. Nothing more painful than for a parent to lose a child, no matter what the circumstances. But we tried to get Mom to do the right thing, we tried to get Gary to do the right thing. You know how they say, 'You can lead a horse to water---'"

"Gary wasn't no *horse!*" flared Angie.

"Yeah, okay, okay, calm down." Bob said, turning to the younger worker, "She's just trying to say that Gary could've chosen the right path; he just chose the wrong. Not your fault."

Angie collected herself. Death, to her, was senseless, albeit a part of life. She had seen death overseas while in the Army; a number of her fellow soldiers were killed in action. Now this kid gets himself killed. Not in action, but in the commission of a senseless crime!

With nothing else to be said, she followed the advice given her all those years ago: *Take a deep breath, hitch up your britches, and carry on, Soldier!*

****

Grief counselors were called in to the Local Office to assist staff members mourning the death of Paulette.

A distraught Arlene was sitting in Kevin Beck's office, along with Bryan. Barely able to control herself, Arlene kept herself together as they spoke. Neither she nor Bryan had slept the night before, and both showed it. No real conversation was made; only small talk, for there was little left to be said.

Fire marshals were still at the remains of the Dahl home, sifting through the wreckage and looking for clues. The bodies had long been taken to the morgue. Paulette and her mother were positively identified through dental records, they were told. An autopsy report was pending, as was the actual cause of the explosion and fire. Still way too early to discuss funeral arrangements.

At the mere mention of funeral, Arlene lost her calm and composure, collapsing onto the floor, screaming and sobbing for all to hear. Wailing so loudly, she had to be tranquilized.

Two days had passed, and things seemed to calm down. The office was quieter, but Nick suspected it to be "the calm before the storm".

He and Paul spoke on the phone; Paul said he was doing fine, enjoying his time off. Nick had filled him in on the recent happenings and said that things were crazy.

"Stay away from here!" he told his friend and coworker, "You're not missing a damn thing." Paul, like all others, was shocked by the news of Paulette's death.

"Give my condolences, will ya?" Paul said.

Nick promised that he would and the two rang off after a couple more minutes of talk. He finished a school collateral on a client, and then walked over to Karen's office. "Here," he said casually, handing over some papers for her approval.

Karen, he saw, was on the phone speaking with an unknown party. Yet he noticed a look of serious concern on his supervisor's face. Normally, Nick would dismiss the look as one of unhappiness regarding a case, but gut instinct told him that something else was wrong.

Karen, obviously, had little concern over the paperwork set before her, but Nick figured that she would review it in time. He left her office and was starting towards the coffee room when someone stopped him. "Did you hear?" the question was asked.

"Hear?" he asked astonishingly, "Hear what?"

"They found Fanny's car on the highway," was the reply, "But she's missing and the cops are looking for her!"

****

"Give me a reason, bitch!"

Mrs. DiCiccio was making the demand, as she looked Fanny Palumbo right in the eye.

It had happened so fast, in fact, that the worker was caught off-guard. Her mind was fixated on her disabled car. Now she was facing, in her mind, Public Enemy Number One--and with barely any chance to retreat.

"I said, *give me a reason!*" Fanny knew full well what the other meant, for in her hand, pointed toward the ground, was a .38-caliber revolver, the small-frame type carried by off-duty cops.

Only, this was no cop! And there was never one around when needed. "I'm just itchin' for the slightest reason to blow a fuckin' hole through your neck!" the disgruntled mom announced.

Fanny instinctively put her hands up as she looked at her nemesis. "Wait," she found her voice, "Calm down, ma'am…let's talk for a second---"

"*SHUT THE FUCK UP!*" spat out Mrs. DiCiccio, "I'm *done with talkin'!* You took my fuckin' kids away…*nobody fucks wit' my kids! Who the fuck you think* you *are, fuckin' wit' me an' my kids?*"

"Mrs. DiCiccio," Fanny tried to reason, "Look---"

"Look, *nothing!*" snarled the other, "Get in the car, bitch!"

Fanny knew that she faced a "fight or flight" situation. It wasn't that she couldn't defend herself, but you don't fight someone with a gun--especially someone as crazy as woman before her! But there was also no chance of flight, for she'd either get hit by a car, or hit by a bullet.

"I said, *get in the goddamned car!!!*" Mrs. DiCiccio raised the gun and pointed it at the worker's chest. "*I'll put a fuckin' bullet between your tits! Better do what I tell ya!*"

Fanny calmly walked towards Mrs. DiCiccio's car. She never took her eyes off of the woman, nor did she put her hands down as she slowly sauntered to the vehicle. "Get in!" she was ordered. Fanny remained calm, yet inside was scared nearly out of her wits. Nevertheless, she still tried to reason with the woman. "Mrs. DiCiccio," she said, "I understand you're upset. I don't blame you, but this is not the way to---"

"Don't tell me *how to do nothin'!"* Mrs. DiCiccio waved her gun in Fanny's direction. "I don't wanna hear what you gotta say! Get in an' shut the fuck up! Blow your goddamned brains all over this road!"

Fanny reached for the passenger door handle and very slowly opened the car door and climbed into the front seat. Fran DiCiccio drove a five-year-old Chrysler convertible whose top was up. All the more, Fanny thought, to conceal her while being held hostage.

The enraged mother drove with one hand, the other keeping her revolver pointed in the worker's direction. She was not a very good driver, for she nearly sideswiped a couple of cars and had to swerve to avoid rear-ending another.

"May I ask where you're taking me?" Fanny inquired.

"You'll see," was the answer, "You'll see and learn what happens to people who fuck wit' my kids!"

They went down the highway, turning off onto a secondary road, proceeded down this road onto a side street. Fanny tried to make a mental note as to their whereabouts. It was just as she was noting the name of a street when she felt a striking blow to her head, and then she saw and felt nothing.

****

"The police found her car."

Jason Palumbo, Fanny's brother, informed the office. "It was sittin' on the shoulder of the highway, hood up, door open."

"And the police are still investigating, I take?" asked Liz Jackson-Harper.

"Investigating?" Jason was incredulous, "They should be fucking *finding* her! Investigate *shit!*"

Jason was standing in Marie Kovacs' office speaking with Marie, Liz, and another CWS. He was a sandy-haired man in his early-forties of medium height with a stocky build slowly turning to fat. His face, not unlike that of his sister, was usually cheery--but not today!

The others shared his frustration. He had been speaking with the detectives repeatedly. The office had informed him of the removal in which his sister was involved, obviously omitting the names and other confidential information.

"'Course, tried her cell phone so many times, I stopped countin'," Jason continued, "They checked her car, didn't find her phone. She's got her phone and I.D., wherever she is…"

Marie wanted to assure Jason that his sister was okay, but she knew herself, even she was not sure. No one was.

The police had towed her car, they were informed. There were signs of foul play: someone had poured something into the car's gas tank--probably water, so it was determined, causing the car to stall. No proof that it was done by whoever had taken her--*if* she was, in fact, taken. Thankfully, no traces of blood were found. The hair fibers were from her own hair; fingerprints her own. Overall, other than the water (or whatever foreign substance) in the fuel line, the car was clean.

Realizing that he could get no closer in finding his sister, Jason left the office. "Let us know, please?" Marie asked.

****

Amy had asked Nick if he was working late. On this day, she hoped that he would be home at the usual time--no late transports, visits, or other. "I should be home on time," he said to her just before leaving for work that morning. "Why, what's up?"

"Nothing," she said shortly, "I'll have dinner ready…just call me when you're leaving, okay?" They kissed, and he promised to call.

He went to the LO and the day officially began for him upon walking in and glancing at the wall clock--9:08 a.m. Checking his calendar, he saw that he had some unfinished paper to be completed, as well as a supervised visit scheduled for later in the day.

The door to Marie's office was closed and had remained so for the last couple of days, Nick had noted. That one of his coworkers might have been…he couldn't bring himself to say "kidnapped"…bothered him deeply. He said a silent prayer for her safe return.

Funeral arrangements had been made for Paulette, Nick read when checking his e-mail. The services for Paulette and her mother were scheduled for the following Saturday, it read, as well as the name of the church at which it would be held, and the time, followed by graveside service and burial, naming the cemetery at which it will take place.

Nick did not know Paulette as closely as he did others within the office, but he did mourn the loss. He doubted that he would attend the services, but did sign the condolence card.

The work day had gone by so quickly that Nick hardly realized that it was nearing the time to go home. He had just returned from a supervised family visit and was completing the contact report when he remembered: *Call Amy.* He did so and informed the other that he was leaving the office in a few minutes.

Nearly an hour later, Nick entered his house amid the aroma of pot roast and potatoes. He kissed Amy and went in to clean up.

Over dinner, some small talk was made. There was something on his sweetheart's mind, he suspected. However, he also knew to give her time; she will get to it. In time.

"Nick," she said, looking his way, "Remember I told you that I was late?"

"Of course."

"I was at the doctor yesterday," she said, "I had some tests done…"

"Okay," he said. She had his full attention now.

"I was thinking maybe we'd have a small blessing in arrival," she went on, "Looks like instead, we have a small *curse…* " she lowered her head and tears ran down her face.

"Honey, what's wrong?" Nick was alarmed.

He reached over to comfort her, "What's the matter? Tell me." By now, Amy had begun shaking as he held her.

"The doctor found…" she said, trying to catch her breath, "a *tumor!*" With that, her body trembled as she was wracked with uncontrollable sobs.

****

A reporter from News12 had been asking questions concerning the missing worker. The LO staff were ordered, per Marie, to *not* speak with anyone from the media. The police were contacted, and officers were dispatched to keep news people away from the office.

Meanwhile, in a secluded location some distance away, Fanny Palumbo was regaining consciousness. Her head aching badly, her eyes were slowly focusing. Obviously not familiar with her surroundings, she slowly remembered her involuntary ride.

She found herself slumped on a dingy floor, and when she turned her painful head, she found herself face-to-face with the toe of a sneaker. A woman's sneaker.

"I oughta take my foot an' kick ya teeth out!" said a voice, and Fanny realized that the owner of the voice was the woman who brought her here.

Okay, she thought, *I'm still alive, but where the hell am I?* She found her own voice and began talking. "My…head…hurts…" the words spilled out slowly.

"A lot more's gonna hurt soon enough!" Mrs. DiCiccio was talking now, "You just don't know what I could do to you! Fuckin' wit' me is one thing, but fuckin' wit' my kids another. I got somethin' for you, bitch…"

"Wait," Fanny said, now realizing her position, "Wait a minute." She got up slowly and every move caused her head to throb sharply. "Lemme just talk to you a sec---"

"Get back on that floor!" Mrs. DiCiccio screamed, raising her gun. "I'm gonna blow a fuckin' hole through your head right fuckin' now, you make another move!"

"Okay, okay, okay…" Fanny conceded and repositioned herself, certain to keep her hands in full view, "Not gonna try anything…just wanna talk to you…"

"You can do all your talkin' right where you are," said Mrs. DiCiccio, "Your *last* talkin', 'cause after that, you gonna be talkin' ta ya Maker!"

There was the sound of a door opening. The enraged mom turned toward the sound and Fanny, knowing discretion to be the better part of valor, wisely remained still. The newcomer was a man, so Fanny had discerned as a male voice was heard.

She could hear whispers between the man and woman, but couldn't make out the words spoke. "Get up!" ordered the female voice.

Fanny lifted herself from the floor, and as she did so got a look at the man. He was a short, swarthy man with dark hair and close-set eyes. Noticing his physique, she guessed that he had been either a bodybuilder or laborer.

"What'cha think, Jimmy?" Mrs. DiCiccio addressed the man, all the while looking at her prey.

"I think," the man called Jimmy said slowly, "that we got us one cornered rabbit. And we're gonna filet her an' serve her up for dinner!"

****

Arlene Rollins put in for a leave of absence and took some time off to mourn her friend and colleague.

In that time, she also went back to her church. Through her pastor, she reunited with old friends and others who had helped her in taking those positive steps from the streets to a better life.

Arlene, it was discovered, had "softened". That is, where she at one point in her life couldn't have cared less about the plight of others, she now found that she did care. She had gone from one extreme to the other, so it seemed--from a life of bad and bitterness to one of caring and compassion.

And so, in this time of hardship and suffering for her late coworker's family, Arlene once again sought the Word of God. Frequent reading of Bible passages and occasional moments of peace and serenity kept her going.

She knew, however, that Paulette's death was no accident. There was no convincing her otherwise--she *knew*. Paulette was sick and tired, she knew, of *being* sick and tired. She--Paulette--had seen and experienced more than one could handle, Arlene knew.

She knew about her father's sudden death. She knew about her brother's sudden death. She knew about her mother's plight and loss of independence.

She knew about Paulette's own loss of independence.

She also knew that there was nothing she, Arlene, could herself do to save her friend from going off the deep end. She saw it in Paulette's eyes: she was beyond saving.

All Arlene could do now was to keep her friend in her prayers, take a deep breath, and venture on. Maybe, she thought, to save other Paulettes of the world. Difficult, if not impossible, she thought. But for all the fighting she had done in her past, this time she was resigned to "fighting the good fight"!

****

"…we're stagnating it. Luckily, it has not metastasized…"

Nick was speaking with Amy's doctor, a Dr. Balfour, who had initially discovered the tumor.

They were in a specialized clinic at St. Clare's Hospital. Dr. Balfour and two specialists, a Dr. Kabib and another doctor whose name Nick failed to remember, were treating Amy.

"We're doing what we can," Dr. Balfour assured him, "She'll have to have specialized treatments. Her family been notified?"

Nick had been in contact with Amy's mother, and told the doctor so. If need be, it was agreed, he will drive to Delaware and bring Mrs. Paladino to the hospital. He had discussed this with Amy, and she agreed also. "How's she doing?" he asked, more for conversation than inquiry.

"She's fine," said the doctor, "You can go in and see her for a few. She's on some strong meds, so she may be a little incoherent."

Nick didn't care how incoherent his lady was. He went in and found Amy resting. Sheets were covering her body; IV tubes connected to her arm. He gently touched her hand and she looked up at him. When she did so, a smile played across her face. "How's it going?" he asked in greeting.

"Question is, how's it going with you?" she countered. Still sharp as a tack, thought Nick.

"I've had better days." said Nick, smiling.

"So have I." Amy shot back.

They spoke for a few minutes. Amy had taken a few days off from work to be examined and undergo procedure, while Nick took some Comp time to care for his love. When she was free and clear, he promised, they will go away together, just the two of them--maybe to the mountains, or Vegas, or wherever she wanted to go.

"Your mom sends her love and prayers." he said to her in conversation.

"My mom," she said, grinning, "Such the one in command. Always the calm, collected one…never lets anything bother her."

Nick didn't disagree. Although Mrs. Paladino seemed a bit apprehensive about her daughter moving away, she always kept a steady demeanor. She was strong that way.

"Any word on your colleague?" Amy asked, "The one that's missing?"

Nick thought quickly. Fanny had still not been found, but he did not want to worry Amy even more. She had enough to worry about.

Much as he hated to lie, he didn't have much of a choice. "The cops traced her," he said, "I think somebody said that she called and the cops traced her number."

"Thank God she's alive." said Amy.

Nick said a silent prayer that his coworker was still among the living. *Wherever you are, Fanny, I pray that you're okay!*

****

Numerous calls to Fanny's cell phone went unanswered. The calls went straight to her voicemail without ringing. Meaning, of course, that her phone was turned off.

Somehow Mrs. DiCiccio had failed to strip her prisoner of her mobile device, for as she checked herself soon after regaining consciousness, Fanny felt the phone in a pocket of her jean jacket. Knowing that reaching out to call 911 would mean sudden, not-so-pretty death, the worker held fast to her thoughts.

Seeing the short, solid man standing before her, Fanny thought that he looked familiar somehow--but her oh-so-splitting headache prevented her from thinking too deeply; she feared that she might have suffered a concussion. Still, she tried to reason her way through. She did not relish the idea of being "fileted".

"Mrs. DiCiccio," she said in a calm, friendly voice, "I know you're upset about all this---"

"Upset?" the enraged mom cut in, *"Upset?? What the fuck do ya know about upset? You sit with your prissy ass in that fuckin'*

Government job snatchin' kids away from their mothers…and you got the fuckin' nerve ta tell me about 'upset'??"

"Mrs. DiCiccio, please," Fanny said, keeping her composure, "Try and understand. All I was doing was what I was asked to---"

"All you were doin' was *ruinin' my life!"* Mrs. DiCiccio cut in again. "You fuckin' *took* my kids away! How the fuck you think *I* feel 'bout my kids gettin' took away? Huh? *YOU THINK IT FEELS GOOD TA HAVE YOUR KIDS TOOK AWAY? DO YA? HUH??"* the words were screamed out.

Still, Fanny tried to reason. "Mrs. DiCiccio," she said, "I never meant to hurt you…I only wanna help you…"

"You can help me by givin' me my kids back!" said the other, her voice lowered an octave, *"That's* how you can help me! But it's too late for that now!"

"It's never too late," said Fanny, trying to buy time, "Please, tell me---"

"Tell ya this," cut in Jimmy, the swarthy stone of a man, now pointing a beefy finger at Fanny, "Bitch, ya shut the fuck up and do as we tell ya! Don' wanna hear no more talk outa ya hole! One more and ya gettin' *another* hole in that pretty little face a' yours. Y'unnerstan'?"

Mrs. DiCiccio raised the gun again, "And

I'm just the one ta give ya that second hole!"

Fanny said nothing. She found herself looking down the barrel of Mrs. DiCiccio's .38. Headache notwithstanding, she tried to remember an old Italian verb that her grandmother had taught her when she was a child. Something that Italians speak among each other when in disagreement.

But she had forgotten it over the years; her grandmother had long since passed away. She sat still, thinking deeply.

****

Gary Holmes' body was laid out for viewing at a church in East Orange. An upbeat Gospel song was playing on the church loudspeakers as people filed by his open casket to pay their final respects.

In the front pew were Gary's mother and brother, as well as scattered relatives—aunts, uncles, cousins. Mrs. Holmes, draped in black, accepted condolences and blessings from those who approached. Many attendees were young people Gary's own age, some making the Sign of the Cross upon seeing their departed friend; one or two others making gang gestures in passing. It was the latter, thought many, who showed no respect for the family.

Also in attendance were workers Angie Franconero and Bob Hendrick. Upon offering their condolences, they knew—and felt—the hostility and animosity directed at them from the family members and friends of Mrs. Holmes. The grieving mother gracefully accepted the offer, and even smiled slightly, but the workers knew that they were not welcome.

Someone, an unidentified observer, made a remark, "You shoulda' done a better job protectin' him. That boy layin' in that box 'cause a you people!"

The two workers looked up and met the eyes of the speaker, whose glare could have blown them both away. Angie wanted to say something in retaliation, but Bob cut off any words with his "We're very sorry for your loss." With that, they made their retreat. No sense in staying where you're not wanted.

In the car, Bob turned to the younger worker. "I know what you were gonna say," he stated, "Sometimes it's just best to just pick and choose your battles. That was *no* place to do battle. Especially with all that hostility in the air."

Angie, in the passenger seat, stared out the windshield while she spoke, "The *nerve* of those people…blamin' *us* for what happened to Gary! Her voice was angry. "They actually think that *we* caused him to go out and rob somebody? And get himself killed in the process?"

"They think we could have done a better job in protecting him," spoke Bob, "They feel—"

"*Protecting* him??" Angie was aghast, "What are we, his *bodyguards* or somethin'? We can't be around these kids twenty-four-seven! We gave him the choices, we gave him the opportunities…*he* made his own choices…"

"Angie, chill out, will ya?" Bob said with emphasis, "Calm down! I'm not arguing with you, I see your point, I understand what you're getting at…"

Angie shut her eyes and silently counted to five. "I'm sorry," she said finally, "I don't mean to bite your head off."

Bob brought his point home. "Listen," he said, his eyes focused on the road ahead as they merged onto Interstate 78, "The job can be a piss hole at times. Some people you can help, but there are others who don't wanna be helped. You may get a family from a well-to-do area, a family from a not-so-well area.

"The ones who will take the necessary steps to better themselves, we're here for them. Even the ones who won't take the steps—well, we're here for them, too. We do everything we can to get these families back on track. We implement programs, therapeutic and otherwise. Some of our families have substance abuse problems, some have criminal histories…we have families who don't speak three words of English—we have to interpret. We have fourteen-and fifteen-year-old girls becoming young mothers; we have mothers with six or seven kids, all from six or seven different fathers! Thirty-five-year-old parents becoming thirty-five-year-old grandparents…

"What I'm getting at is: you take the job for what it is! Nobody said that this was the easiest job in the world. It's an interesting job, but it damn sure ain't *easy!* Okay, so Gary couldn't be saved—or protected, as mentioned. Despite all that's happened, we only did what we could for Gary, and all else was on him.

"So quit takin' so much to heart!" Bob concluded. "Take a deep breath, mourn the loss for a time, and then move forward. That's what this job's all about—moving *forward!*"

****

Paul Zahorsky was enjoying his time off. Or at least, trying.

He had been married four years before he was appointed to the Division. His wife, Wendy, forever nagged him to quit and go back to teaching, which she thought was more rewarding.

"Once you've got tenure," she had said, "you can go back to school, complete your degree and become a clinician. Or a therapist. Why travel all over the state to service those kids?" she went on. "You can service kids within a school!"

Paul had repeatedly explained to his wife that he liked what he did. He liked the autonomy and diverseness he experienced.

The marriage was on the rocks, and Paul knew it. He and Wendy had an eleven-year-old daughter, and Paul worshiped her immensely. Marriage counseling had been tried, and things had improved for a time. However, the novelty of it was wearing off on Paul and Wendy Zahorsky. Much as he liked being home with his wife and daughter, the relationship was strained.

The first serious thoughts of divorce had crossed his mind several weeks before.

Wendy, he thought, was too materialistic and manipulative. Seemed that she wouldn't be happy unless her husband worked a suit-and-tie job as some corporate flunky.

Today he was working in the basement of their home. Paul had made a portion of the basement into a wood shop—woodworking was his hobby, and he was building bar stools.

Wendy was upstairs watching some reality show on TV while Emily, their daughter, was chatting with her friends on *Facebook*.

Paul had not felt like his usual self all day; he felt somewhat sluggish and run-down. *Guess I must've ate something doesn't agree with me,* he thought. He had just cut and measured a pair of wooden rods for stool legs. Using a belt sander on the countertop, he shaped each piece to design perfection.

Sanding done, he carefully examined his work. Any imperfections were remedied with a piece of fine-grit sandpaper. He was reaching for a small carving tool when he realized he was in trouble. The right side of his body went numb, and the stool leg he was holding fell to the floor. Two seconds after which he collapsed with a heavy thud to the floor. His mouth open, yet no words could be spoken. His right side having no feeling or movement, Paul helplessly was writhing N the floor, unable to get up or speak.

"*The fuck you lookin' at, bitch??!!*"

Fanny, in her thinking, did not realize that she was staring in Mrs. DiCiccio's direction. Now, the enraged woman was raising the gun again and pointing it directly at her. "I said, *what the fuck you lookin' at??!!*"

The hostage regained her bearings and quickly put her hands up to shoulder level, "N-nothing…" she blurted out, "Nothing, Mrs. DiCiccio. I…"

"You *what?*" demanded the other, "You…*what?* Thinkin' of a way ta run? Fight me? Get my gun? *What, bitch?*" She moved closer and Fanny instinctively took a step back, as if to keep a distance. "DON'T FUCKIN' MOVE!" screamed Mrs. DiCiccio, "STAY THERE!! One more step and you fuckin' die, understand?"

Fanny remained rooted. Her hands still up, she spoke gently, "Mrs. DiCiccio, can I ask you a question?"

"What the hell ya want?"

"I told you that I understood your anger," said Fanny, "and I know that you want your children, but I can help you…could you at least let me help you? There is positive in this, and I'm sure we——"

"Don't fuckin' talk to me 'bout positive!" snarled Mrs. DiCiccio, "You *took* whatever 'positive' there was away." She stepped closer and touched the muzzle of the revolver against Fanny's forehead. Fanny, sweating with fear, felt the cold blue steel on her skin. "I could blow that little brain a' yours clean outa your head right now." The words came out low, an octave above a whisper, "And nobody'd be the smarter. Fuck wit' *me,* huh bitch?"

Fanny knew to just shut up and wait it out. Hopefully, the enraged parent will calm down enough. Slowly, Mrs. DiCiccio's finger unhooked its way from the trigger, and as it did so Fanny relaxed ever-so-slightly. The gun was also brought off of her forehead and the captor, looking at the scared woman squatting before her, shook with laughter. "Got the shit scared outa ya, huh?" she laughed. "I bet you're pissin' an' shittin' your panties now, thinkin' you was breathin' ya last breath there!"

If the thought had not occurred before, it did now. Fanny had to pee. But there was no way she was going to convey this to that lunatic in front of her. Not now, at least.

Realizing that she might be living the last moments of her life, she silently prayed. No churchgoer was Fanny, but she did believe in God. She prayed silently, asking forgiveness for all her past sins—and if this *was* her time to go, prayed that it would be quick, painless, and that the journey Upstairs be a pleasant one.

It's been said that when you are faced with death, your whole life passes before you. Fanny, suddenly, saw her late grandmother before her.

Her *Nonna* was there, watching from a short distance. She stood, speaking with her eyes: *Nipote*, she said calmly, *la speranza e l'ultima morire…*

That's it! Fanny thought almost excitedly, *Those are the words* mi nonna *taught me! La speranza e l'ultima morire!* Hope is the last to die!

Facing her captor, Fanny spoke, "Mrs. DiCiccio," she said, feeling somewhat safer now, "Remember I told you about my being able to help you? I can still do that. If you want, I can make arra—"

"And what the hell you think *you* can do for me?" the words came out like daggers.

"You'll get your children back," Fanny said, "Please, just listen a minute—"

"Thought I tol' ya ta shut the fuck up!" Jimmy cut in.

"Just listen a minute—*please.*" Fanny knew

that she was taking her life into her hands by talking, but decided that if she had to die, she would die fighting to save herself. "Just please, please, please, listen a minute. That's all I ask of you."

The briefest of silences followed. "You got one minute," was the reply, "Whadaya want?"

"You said your positive was taken away," Fanny spoke, "Well, I don't think it was. All I'm trying to do is help. I know that you've had some bad luck lately, but I want to do what I can to help turn it around.

"I may die here. You could kill me right where I stand," she went on, "But if I die, so goes the hope in your life. And as long as nobody gets hurt, hope is still around. Try and keep that hope alive, Mrs. DiCiccio. *La speranza e l'ultima morire! Per picere,* Mrs. DiCiccio!"

The woman's eyes widened as she looked at Fanny. *"Sai parlare Italiano?"* she asked.

"Si parla poco Italiano." Fanny answered, and that was all the Italian she knew.

Mrs. DiCiccio turned away momentarily. She looked over at Jimmy and they spoke in hushed tones.

Taking a very risky chance, Fanny reached into her pocket for her cell phone. Knowing that to use it would mean sudden death, she prayed that she had remembered to keep it on silent mode. She pushed the power button and hoped that the phone would remain silent. Slowly removing her hand, she remained still as Jimmy grabbed her by the upper arm. "Let's go!" he ordered, "Takin' ya someplace!"

■■

The stress and fatigue were beginning to take their toll on Nick. He was tired physically and emotionally.

Despite such, he had to stay strong for his Amy. After a series of examinations and treatments, she was making weekly trips to a therapist for shots of chemo. There were no physical changes in Amy's appearance; she was keeping her weight and no hair had fallen out, but she was tired. Nick saw it in her eyes.

The tiredness followed him to work. He methodically caught up on his case paper as if on automatic pilot. Not as talkative as his usual self, when his colleagues approached him, his words were vague and the "closed" persona remained with him throughout the morning.

Already weighted down with the issues concerning Amy, Paulette, and Fanny, he stared at the phone on his desk when it rang. Snatching up the receiver, he answered, "Yeah?" with a twinge of annoyance in his voice.

"Nick," said Karen, "Could you come to my office, please?" There was a tone of urgency in his boss's voice. After the briefest of acknowledgments, Nick hung up. He just wanted to sit at his desk and brood for a while, but his gut told him that the summons to Karen's office was something of importance.

"Close the door." Karen said upon his arrival. He did so and turned to face her. Pain had crossed the supervisor's face, and whatever it was, Nick knew, was not good.

"We just got a call," Karen began, "Paul's in the hospital."

A look of apprehension overcame Nick. "*What??*" he nearly shouted. "What the hell…"

"They're saying he had a stroke," Karen went on, "It's bad…"

Nick, when faced with overwhelming news, would look down and pinch the bridge of his nose with his thumb and fingers. He sat in a chair and did just so as he asked in a muffled voice, "How did it…?" he could not finish the question.

"Far as we know," Karen said, "his wife found him on the floor in their basement. He was doing some woodworking or something…she heard a loud clatter, asked if he was all right. When he didn't answer, she went down and found him on the floor, his eyes were open but he was dazed and drooling. She called 911 and when they got there, determined that he had had a stroke."

"How bad?"

"No movement on his right side," Karen said in a sorrowful voice, "Speech is nil. They're still doing tests."

Nick sat awhile to let the news sink in. he had not told Karen about Amy's condition, and now this, along with all else!

"I know you're going through a lot now…" she said after a few minutes.

Hoo boy! Nick thought, *you couldn't begin to know…*

"…I need you to take over some of Paul's assignments," continued Karen, "Get with Lisa and see what Paul had ongoing in terms of visits, court papers, whatever. See what you can do in the interim. Let me know?"

Nick nodded slightly. Paul was—*is*—a good friend as well as coworker. He never seemed to let anything rankle him, but Nick thought that the latest incident involving that crazy mom who falsely accused him of rape might have done him in.

"I'll talk to Lisa, see what's doin', and get back with you ASAP." he promised.

"Thanks." Karen replied, "There's a card going around the office. Maybe you wanna bring it to him after everyone signs it?" she inquired.

Nick agreed. He left Karen's office and went over to see Paul's supervisor, Lisa Morales.

Lisa looked up at Nick upon his arrival and said, "I can't tell you how much I appreciate this, Nick. You okay?"

He was *not* okay, but decided that he would function as best he could, given everything. "Yeah, thanks Lisa. Whatta ya got?"

Nick had known Lisa for the past three years, as she had transferred from a Southern region LO. Upon her promotion to Unit Supervisor, she was assigned to the Adoption Unit. Lisa and Nick had had a touch of friction in the past, but it was hashed out. They had sized each other up, so to speak, and although she was a Sup and he an AFSW, it was determined that—titles aside—they were evenly matched in temperament and wit.

"Paul had a couple of visits in his work plans," Lisa began, handing him some forms. "This one here—the Bryce visit—is in limbo;

Mr. Bryce is in jail. Doubt that one's gonna happen anytime soon.

"This other one's for Thursday," she went on. "Pending, of course, confirmation. Mom's gonna need to come in for an SAE. We need to get her in here soon as possible. You got any time today?"

"Think maybe I can squeeze her in this afternoon." affirmed Nick.

"Great!" said Lisa, "I'll give her a call, you go an' get her, bring her in?"

"Who's the worker?"

"Betty, but she's in training."

"Okay," Nick said, "Let me know ASAP?"

"You got it."

Nick stopped off and briefed Karen on Lisa's requests. After a heartfelt "Thanks" from both supervisors, he returned to his desk. He added the new assignments onto his calendar and sat silently in thought: *When it rains, it pours. When it shits, it's diarrhea!*

∎∎∎

"We've got a track. Possible hit!" Detective Fitzgerald Scott of the State

Police was monitoring the SPEN database.

The SPEN—State Police Emergency Network—was a computer tool utilized to track down wanted fugitives and missing persons. A red signal had illuminated on the screen; the State Police, given Fanny Palumbo's cell phone number, had tracked it via GPS.

"Looks like that industrial area in Woodbridge," Det. Sergeant Edmund Shea said, looking at the signal, "Get on that thing, advise Woodbridge P.D., let 'em know we're on our way!"

Scott made a note of the location and called in an "all alert" to Woodbridge and surrounding departments. He, Shea, and two other detectives raced to the location in unmarked cars with portable strobes flashing and sirens blaring.

Upon arrival some fifteen minutes later, detectives from Woodbridge and about a dozen uniformed cops met them. Sergeant Shea quickly briefed the Woodbridge police captain on the situation and the uniforms were ordered to take positions around the warehouse perimeter.

Guns drawn and all cops poised, Scott took the loudspeaker: *Whoever's inside,* he announced, *State Police. Open the door and step out with your hands up!*

Silence followed. Scott made the announcement again, followed by: *This building is surrounded. Step outside with your hands up!*

More silence. The Woodbridge captain nodded to a couple of officers, who began firing rounds of tear gas through a window. Four other cops broke open a door with a steel battering ram and the officers entered quickly, shouting, *"Police! Come out! Now!"*

They were at least five minutes too late. Their target, they discovered, had left through a separate passageway.

■■

"How is he?"

Nick had gone to the hospital to check on his friend and colleague, Paul. He ran into Paul's wife in the hall as she was going for coffee.

"He's responsive, somewhat," Wendy answered, "He can see and hear, but can't move or speak." She had been crying, Nick thought as he looked at Wendy. Her eyes were red and raw; it had not been a good time for her.

Nick walked into the room and found his friend laying on his back, facing the ceiling. There were tubes emerging from his arm and linked to an electronic machine. Trying not to notice, he made eye contact with Paul. "Hey, dude," he said in greeting, "I leave you alone for just five minutes and you get in trouble? Can't I even *trust* ya?" It was his and Paul's own way of making light of circumstances.

There was the slightest hint of a smile as Paul looked at Nick. But with that smile, he knew another look. One of fear. Paul's eyes, to Nick, seemed to say, "Look at this, isn't this just terrible?" Nick in turn did his best to keep it calm and encouraging.

He did not tell Paul about the goings-on at the office, lest Paul get further upset. He did, however, say that he—Nick—would cover for him in his absence. "So don't you worry," he said, "I got it all taken care of. Lisa and I went over everything…just want you should rest up. And for God's sake, *get better* or I'm gonna have to pull you up outa that bed and *drag* you back to wellness!" This was followed by a chuckle, and even Paul smiled.

Leaving the hospital after some parting words, Nick sat in his car and thought about

Paul. His prognosis was not good. Aphasia was bad enough, but he could not even move the right side of his body. Which meant Paul would no longer be able to do even the simplest of things—like speak, walk, drive a car, or write his own name. Wendy was gonna have a lot on her hands, on top of raising their daughter!

Nick started the engine, pulled out of the parking lot and headed home. Driving, he now thought of Amy. She was undergoing some treatments at a center and the treatments were sucking the energy out of his usually vibrant lady. She had gone back to work, and was performing her job as normal. Nevertheless, she looked and sounded tired. She *was* tired.

To compensate, Nick took over some of the domestics. He cooked more meals and ran more errands. He liked to cook, but had not done much since Amy moved in with him. Now, he saw, he was not involuntarily performing the function. He cooked what Amy liked to eat, and felt appreciated watching her devour whatever he prepared.

But now with the chemo, rather than keeping the food down, Amy vomited it up. She apologized profusely to Nick, and he understood; yet it still hurt to prepare meals for her, only for her to vomit shortly thereafter. Quietly, he held her in his arms as she cried.

He also thought of the time he would need in going to the doctor. Given his own work schedule—and now that of Paul's—he determined that he would be doubly busy. Karen and Lisa would both just have to understand.

Speaking of which, he had not even *told* Karen!

Nick had been so preoccupied with the goings-on concerning his colleagues, he totally neglected to let Karen know about Amy. His philosophy being that it was his and Amy's problem!

Arriving home, he took a deep breath and exhaled audibly as he opened the door and entered. He found Amy seated on the living room couch, the TV on. "How's Paul?" she asked in greeting.

Nick did not want to tell Amy Paul's true prognosis; it would only make her more miserable. "He's okay." he said, "The doctors are still running some tests."

Amy was about to ask another question, but hers was interrupted by a news story:

"...State Police are combing the Woodbridge area in search of a Division worker who is missing and said to have been kidnapped..."

****

On a cool day of which the sun played peek-a-boo behind clouds, several staff and others assembled at Mount Holiness Church for the funeral services of Paulette Dahl and her mother, Mrs. Antonia Dahl.

The church was packed to the rafters—Standing Room Only. Mrs. Dahl's pastor was one of several presiding over the services, as were others from the community who knew and loved the Dahl family.

There were no caskets. It was requested that the remains of Paulette and her mom be cremated; their ashes placed within an urn, which sat atop a pew, as the services were underway.

Among Paulette's colleagues in attendance were LO Manager Marie Kovacs; Case Work Supervisors Kevin Beck and Annette Martinez; Unit Supervisors Bryan Taylor and Karen Emory; and workers Bob Hendrick, Arlene Rollins and several others to bid farewell and pay their respects.

A close family friend of the Dahls was asked to deliver the eulogy. In the middle of doing so, this person was so overcome with grief he had to be helped off the lectern. He and his family had known Mr. and Mrs. Dahl for his entire life—they were, in a sense, his "second parents"; Paulette a sister.

Arlene, in her seat, kept her face buried in her hands and sobbed as quietly as she could. She felt an arm around her and knew the touch to be one of sympathy, yet continued sobbing nevertheless.

Following the services, many of the mourners followed the procession from the church to the cemetery, located some thirty miles away. A small hole had been dug at the Dahl plot, and the urn was placed within. Of this, Bryan was the only member of the Division who attended; Arlene was too distraught. She could not bear seeing someone buried—she had seen that play too many times herself!

■ ■

"Saw a blue car…went barrelin' outa here like a bat outa hell!"

The disheveled-looking man with the

scruffy beard was talking to the detectives. He was a homeless man, pushing a supermarket shopping cart that contained all his worldly possessions.

"You get a plate number, or what?" Detective Scott demanded. He thought that he was just wasting precious time talking to this vagabond.

"No plate, but was a blue Chrysler," said the man.

"Blue Chrysler," Scott mimicked.

"Was a convertible, if that'll help." added the man.

"Was the top up or down?" Scott asked harshly.

"Up."

"How many people in the car?"

"Seen two. Man and woman. Look like they was in a hurry an' wanted ta get somewhere—"

"You only saw *two* people?" cut off Scott.

"All I seen. They was—"

"Anybody in the backseat? Anybody else?" Scott cut him off again.

The man looked down and shook his head, "That's all I seen, officer. Like I said, they went flyin' past—"

"Which way did they go?" the detective cut him off again.

"Down that way," he answered, "Turned left

an' went squealin' away like they had a hot date."

Scott relayed the information to Sergeant Shea. The officers recorded the information to be inputted on the SPEN. It was a long shot, but it was a lead.

There was also proof that the warehouse building had most recently been occupied. A fresh cigarette butt was found near the door; the officers bagged and tagged the stogie for analysis.

Back at the State Police troop, there were three separate messages from Jason, Fanny's brother. Shea returned the call. No, they had not found his sister yet, Jason was told. Yes, they are working on finding her…we'll let you know as soon as we have something…yada, yada, yada…

Scott, meanwhile, checked the database. "I think we got a hit," he said to Shea, "Blue Chrysler convertible…there is one registered to a Francesca DiCiccio."

"DiCiccio's got the girl," Shea mused, "We already figured that."

"But did you figure who the guy was with her?" asked another detective, walking into the room.

"Well, don't keep us waiting," Shea said impatiently, "Spill it!"

"James 'Jimmy V' Valenza…son of

Dominick 'Heavy Legs' Valenza!"

The other cops stiffened. Jimmy V was just as ruthless as his father. Law enforcement authorities knew stories of loan-sharking, extortion, bodies found in landfills and trash compactors—some bodies never found at all!

"We need to find that fucking car," Shea said, a desperate tone in his voice, "And quick!"

■■■

Fran DiCiccio did not pay much attention to her driving.

Nearly running down an old bum as she exited the warehouse, she narrowly missed a parked car as she drove down the narrow side street.

Turning onto Route 9 toward Sayreville, she took the three-lane road at better than 70 mph, oblivious to the traffic around her. She continued her maniacal driving, swerving around slower moving cars as if they were parked.

Her luck ran out when a police cruiser from

Old Bridge Township flew up behind her, the cop car's strobes flashing its red and blue for all to see. Looking in her mirror, Mrs. DiCiccio mouthed, "OH, *SHIIIIIT!*"

Jimmy, in the passenger seat, began yelling at her, "Tol' ya ta slow the fuck down, di'n't I? *Why the fuck don'cha LISTEN, ya stupid cunt!!*"

She did not pull over immediately—and in so refusing, was further infuriating the cop on her tail. Knowing that one cop could turn into even more, she finally rolled the Chrysler to the shoulder of the highway.

"What the hell's your damn problem?" the cop yelled at her upon approaching the window, "You havin' a baby or somethin'?"

Apparently, the officer had not gotten the message that this woman was a wanted person. He snatched her license and registration from her hand and stormed back to his cruiser.

Jimmy sat silently, staring through the car's windshield. Fanny, in the back seat, kept quiet during the ride. One word, she knew, and she could be dead meat, cop or no cop!

Mrs. DiCiccio, a wild look in her eyes, kept staring at the side-and rear-view mirrors. She saw in the distance another set of flashing lights, and knew it was another officer responding to back up the one who'd stopped her.

It was at this time, when all else failed in her mind, that she decided to slip the car in Drive, and take off, flooring the accelerator!

■■■

Arlene Rollins returned to work, insisting on moving forward.

Obviously, it had not been an easy week for her. But, as she had been taught: *When the going gets tough...*

She was tough, she knew, and she had to get going! On her desk before her was a thick case file. It was one of a family that had been in the system for years—a single mom, six children, all of whom are in foster care.

Reading the note attached to the file, Arlene discovered that the case was reassigned to her; the previous worker had been transferred to the Intake Unit. Arlene was to follow up on the fact-findings, court reviews, and schedule some MVRs. Some of the children were not living together, as it was; they were in different placements in different parts of the state.

Picking up the phone on her desk, she called one, then another caregiver, making plans to go to the homes and check on the youngsters' well-being, as well as the conditions of the respective homes.

She remained busy as much as possible, and in doing so was able to forget her own sadness. She checked in with Bryan and advised him that she would be out in the field on a couple of MVRs.

Signing out a state car from motor pool, she drove to a modest two-story home located about forty-five minutes from the LO. She had never met the caregiver, nor the children, but she knew of the case. She introduced herself as the new caseworker and spoke with the children.

"What happened to Helen?" they asked. Helen was the previous worker.

"Helen's been reassigned," Arlene answered in a friendly voice, "I'm gonna be taking over your case."

"Oh." was the reply.

"How you guys doin' in school?" Arlene asked. Actually, it was two boys and a girl.

"Good." they said innocently. The children were eleven, nine, and eight in ages. The nine-year-old had recently been diagnosed with dyslexia and had significant reading difficulties.

Arlene went on to speak with the caregiver while the children went about their business. The caregiver said that the two younger children were a bit hyperactive at times, but otherwise well-mannered and obedient.

"Anything going on with their mother?" asked the caregiver.

"Nothing new just now," answered Arlene, "I'm gonna see her tomorrow; she has to be in court this week."

Arlene asked if the caregiver or the children needed anything. Nothing was needed, said the caregiver. She looked in on the kids and said goodbye, wished everyone well and left.

After a quick stop at a Dunkin' Donuts, Arlene drove to the other resource home. Again, she introduced herself to the people within. The children here were older. Teenagers.

"When coul' we go home?" was the first question from one of the kids. Arlene noted that this one, a fourteen-year-old girl, dressed provocatively.

"That depends on your mom," Arlene said levelly, "Your mom needs to finish her program and do a couple other things before we can let you go home."

The girl responded with a roll of eyes and sucking teeth. It was going to be difficult with this bunch.

Along with the fourteen-year-old were two other children: a boy, thirteen, and another girl, sixteen. "I know you wanna be back with your mom," said Arlene, trying to win their confidence, "But she needs to get some things done before we can send you home."

"That fuckin' judge can *kiss my ass!*" yelled the sixteen-year-old girl, the eldest of the children, "The fuck do he know 'bout what my mom gotta go through? What about what *we* gotta go through? Fuckin' white trash motherfucker!"

Arlene was about to ask the girl to watch her language, but was halted by the caregiver, a heavyset black woman. "You don't talk that way in my house!" she hollered, "In *my* house, you show some *respect!*" The caregiver moved in front of the foul-mouthed girl. "Don'choo *ever* lemme hear you talkin' like that in my house again, you unnerstan'?

The girl stood silently and rolled her eyes. "You can roll 'em eyes all you wan' but'choo sho' cain't shoot 'em!" the caregiver remarked. She turned to the worker, "I'm sorry fo' her behavior," she said, "She jus' have a attitu' problem at times." Now she turned back to the girl, "And *you* got somethin' ta say t' the lady, too."

The girl mumbled a barely audible "Sorry", but made no eye contact with the worker. It was decided that Arlene would wrap it up and head back to the office. She handed her business card to the caregiver, wished everyone well and departed.

Driving back to the LO, her cell phone rang. It was Bryan.

"You're not gonna believe it," he said shortly, "But those kids you just saw, their mom's supposed to be in court soon, right?"

"Yea, Thursday, from what I understand."

"Probably gonna need to hold off on that now." said Bryan.

"Why?"

"Mom was just arrested. Possession with intent to distribute, within 1,000 feet of a school!"

"Damn!" spat out Arlene.

"County, 7 Gs, no ten."

Arlene knew the terminology. Mom was being held in the County jail on $7,000 bail with no 10-percent option. And the kids were asking, *When could they go home?*

- -

Nick and Amy were watching the news unfold on their TV.

"*...Police have swarmed the Industrial section of Woodbridge in search of the missing Child Protective Services worker who is believed to have been kidnaped by an angry parent who had had her children removed by the Division...*"

"Oh, my God!" Amy said, her eyes glued to the screen, "I sure hope they find her!"

"Me too." Nick responded.

"*...At this time, police are not speculating whether or not they are close to finding the worker, or the parties who allegedly kidnaped her. A police spokesman has told News 12 that every possible lead is being investigated...*"

Nick knew that statement to mean: *The police don't have jack shit and they're looking to the public for help!*

The news story was barely finished when Amy suddenly got up from the couch and ran toward the bathroom. She had not yet reached the toilet when Nick heard her gagging and vomiting. His heart sank.

After a couple of minutes, he knew, she would run the tap, wash her face and clean up the area. However, he never heard the water run. There was silence.

He waited another two minutes, then hollered out to her, "Honey?" he called, "You all right?"

There was no response.

He repeated the inquisition. Still no answer. Concerned, he walked to the bathroom and found Amy, lying unconscious, on the bathroom floor, vomit flowing from her mouth.

■■

Fran DiCiccio drove the blue Chrysler furiously down Route 9.

The officer who stopped her had barely settled into his cruiser when she took off leaving tire smoke and black marks in the roadway. The second cruiser paused briefly, to check on his colleague, and then took off after the fleeing car.

With speeds approaching ninety, the Chrysler swerved from one lane to the other, dodging slower traffic. The black-and-white unit was fast closing in on its prey.

Taking a hard-right turn onto a side road, Mrs. DiCiccio sideswiped a New Jersey

Transit bus, which was stopped to discharge a passenger. The bus driver, getting off to assess the damage to his bus, was himself nearly run down by a pursuing police car.

Flying down the two-lane road at a suicidal clip, the panicked mom hit the brake and made a left turn onto another road. As she did so, the Chrysler lost traction and drifted toward the right, landing onto the grassy shoulder.

Flooring the gas, she took off again, the car's front wheels spinning furiously, leaving clouds of dust and tire smoke in its wake.

The pursuing unit, its Police Interceptor engine working overtime, hooked the sharp turn with a screech of tires. Its back end fishtailed as the turn was completed.

Three more police cruisers joined in the pursuit, their sirens blaring and strobes flashing. The Chrysler barreled aimlessly with the law in its wake.

Jimmy, in the front seat, turned to the crazy woman driving the car. A look of fear had crossed his face. "Fuckin' *Christ,* bitch! You wanna fuckin' *kill* us? Fuck's wrong wit' ya, *stupid cunt!!!*" he screamed at her.

Fanny, in the back seat, was muted with sheer terror. Staring out the windshield, she half-expected a car to cross their path at any second. Glancing at the car's speedometer, she saw the needle approaching one hundred. Given the maniacal speeds, coupled with a bunch of cops in pursuit, Fanny barely felt the hot wetness trickling down her jeans!

Mrs. DiCiccio yanked the car suddenly off the road, onto yet another roadway. The impact of the sudden turn knocked Fanny into the C-pillar, just behind the driver side window. Two hard knocks to the head would render a person unconscious—and Fanny, while not losing consciousness, saw stars as she put her hand to the impacted area.

Taking the road at nearly ninety, Mrs. DiCiccio did not have time to negotiate the curve to the right. Unable to slow down in time, the car drifted around the curve, all four wheels losing traction. Trying blindly to correct, she over-corrected, and the car went one way, then another. At ninety miles per hour, the car slid sideways for several yards, then spun completely into a 360-degree skid. Blue smoke from the tires blinded the occupants, and almost instantly, they felt a hard jolt as the car banged against something hard in the ground.

The smoke barely clearing, the panicked mom tried to restart the vehicle as the cops jumped from their cruisers, guns drawn, and stormed the now-disabled car. Screams of: "GET OUT!!" "SHOW US YOUR

HANDS!!!" emitted from the officers.

Mrs. DiCiccio pulled the .38 from a pocket. She pointed the revolver at Fanny and cocked the hammer. "I might die here, but I'm takin' you wit' me, bitch!" she said in a clenched voice. She reached back and grabbed Fanny by the upper arm. "One little sound and you're done!"

Two officers approached the car, their weapons pointed at both Mrs. DiCiccio and Jimmy. "Drop the gun!" one of them demanded.

"*You* drop the fuckin' guns!" demanded the crazy mom, "Or I put a bullet in Miss Wet Pants here!" Now it was realized that Fanny had peed on herself.

"Get out of the car! *Now!*" one of the cops screamed, reaching for the door handle. As he opened the door, Mrs. DiCiccio pressed her gun against Fanny's temple.

"Don't you fuckin' *dare!*" she said, "I'll shoot her! I swear ta God I'll fuckin' *shoot* this bitch!"

Another officer, appearing from nowhere, yanked open the passenger side door. Moving quickly, he and a second cop grabbed Jimmy, pulled him roughly from the car and wrestled him to the ground. "Don't move, asshole!" they screamed at him. "Don't *fucking* move!"

Briefly distracted by this, Mrs. DiCiccio

saw that she was cornered. Turning, she pulled the trigger and the shot caught Fanny in the upper chest.

This was followed by more shots, these fired from the officers' weapons. A discharge caught the distraught mother in her midsection; she felt the blow puncturing one of her lungs. She felt another bullet tearing through her neck. After the feel of a third shot through her chest, Francesca DiCiccio felt no more.

■■

"She's coming to."

Nick was riding in the ambulance with the paramedic. An oxygen mask was over Amy's face as she lay on the stretcher.

Upon noticing her, Nick immediately dialed 911. When the paramedics arrived, he explained her condition.

"Most likely a side effect of the chemo," said one of the EMTs treating Amy, "How much was administered?"

Nick told him. Siren blaring, the ambulance roared down the street, en route to the hospital.

Amy was brought in and a triage nurse attended to her almost immediately. By now, she had gained full consciousness and although remaining still, her eyes darted around, as if to say: *What happened?*

Nick informed her that she had passed out. He did not mention the chemo, or the possible effects thereof. "Just relax, baby," he assured her, "Everything's okay. I think you're just overtired and in need of rest."

She said nothing, but asked with her eyes: *Why did I pass out?*

Nick did not want to lie—he hated lying. But seeing the look in the eyes of his love, he felt he had little choice but to skate around the truth. "I think," he said, choosing his words, "that you are pretty worn down with the worries, the doctor visits, and the stresses of work…" He did not want to avert his eyes, for she knew he would be holding something back. Which she hated more than anything!

But she knew. It was not any stresses or worries, it was the chemo. Fortunately for Nick, she was not angry.

Amy found her voice, and they spoke for a few more minutes, mostly small talk. A woman appeared, seemingly from nowhere.

"Hi," she said in greeting, "I'm Dr. Phelan. I understand you passed out earlier." She was reading Amy's chart.

Nick excused himself to step out. "I shan't be far, my good lady." he said, mimicking a British accent.

He went out into the hall and gathered his thoughts. *If I smoked,* he thought, *I probably would'a smoked half a pack by now!* He had quit smoking over five years ago, and never touched another cigarette since. He dwelled further: *I smoked, and I'm healthy as a newborn; she never smoked in her entire life, and* she *possibly gets cancer? It ain't right! It-just-ain't-right, dammit!*

His thoughts were interrupted by a commotion at the Emergency entrance. Several cops, along with some paramedics, were frantically wheeling in a bandaged patient. Looking toward the noise, Nick saw from his POV that the person being wheeled in somehow looked familiar. The person *was* someone familiar. *Oh, shit! That's Fanny!!!*

■■ ■ ■

Police from Old Bridge Township, along with State Police and neighboring law enforcement personnel, were assessing the post-shooting damage.

Ambulances were radioed and en route; the roadway closed off to all traffic.

Jimmy Valenza was taken into custody. The police knew of his long rap sheet and as it turned out, he had a couple of Federal warrants for his arrest.

Francesca DiCiccio's bullet-riddled body was dragged from the car; her .38 revolver seized and invoiced by the detectives.

Fanny Palumbo, it was confirmed, was the innocent hostage. Her unconscious body was soaked with urine and blood, the latter a result of a direct shot from Mrs. DiCiccio's gun, along with line-of-fire grazing from the officers' rounds. She sustained gunshot wounds to her right chest, shoulder and upper arm, along with a concussion from being pistol-whipped.

The Chrysler, now bullet-holed and its interior a crimson mess, was towed to the police impound for further investigation.

Detectives Shea and Scott arrived and briefed the local authorities on the investigation. Upon the bodies being taken to their respective destinations—Jimmy to the County jail; DiCiccio to the morgue; Fanny to the hospital—the scene was cleaned up and slowly, the cops dispersed.

Fanny's brother Jason was called by Sergeant Shea. The detective informed the other that his sister had been found. Yes, she was still alive, Jason was told, and en route to the hospital.

A news helicopter, hovering over the scene, told of an "ongoing police investigation" in Old Bridge. "It is speculated," the reporter announced, "that it may have connection with the missing State worker." The news camera zoomed in on a shot of the blue Chrysler, being winched onto a flatbed truck. "We hope to have more details shortly." the reporter concluded, "Now back to you in the newsroom."

With a rushed arrival to the hospital, an unconscious Fanny Palumbo could not be aware of how lucky she was to be alive! Nor was she aware of the coworker standing not twenty feet away!

■■■ ■ ■■

LO Manager Marie Kovacs felt bewitched and besieged!

Phone calls from disgruntled parents screaming about visits with their children; Kathy Blasi, the Area Office Director and Marie's immediate boss hounding her ass about reports from Unit and Case Work Supervisors concerning SARs and other paper; one worker dead, another missing, yet another in the hospital and incapacitated!

Still in spite of it all, she had to run the ship. In a meeting with Case Work Sups Kevin Beck and Annette Martinez, she was asking for an update on a few cases, soon to be transferred to another LO. "Where are we on the Brauner case?" she asked Kevin.

"The mom's in a mental institution indefinitely," Kevin answered, "Dad's taking the kids and relocating to North Carolina. He says that he's found a good school for them…says that he got a job offer down there, working for Toyota at one of their car plants."

"And Mom?" Marie went on, "How's she taking this news?"

"Angie says that she seems as she doesn't really care," answered Kevin, "She's in a world of her own, so it seems. Last Family Team meeting, she just sat there like a lump of clay. Apparently, she just doesn't give a damn what happens with her family."

Marie looked down and briefly shook her head. Turning to Annette, she asked about a couple of different cases.

Annette cleared her throat before speaking, "Miss B got kicked out of her parents' house," she stated, "Her screenings have either yielded dirty urine, or she just doesn't show up when asked to. Every time we schedule, she makes some excuse, 'Oh, I've got a job interview…' 'I have a doctor's appointment…' whatever. What, two weeks ago, we sent a worker out to pick her up at where she was staying. She slammed the door in the poor worker's face!"

"So now, I understand she's down in South Jersey, right?" Marie asked.

"Supposedly." Annette answered, "We have yet to determine, but from my understanding, she's staying with an old boyfriend—one of her kids' fathers, I believe."

And probably another drug user, thought Marie. "We need to get the packages together. Gather up everything on those cases and get 'em over to Clerical. Make sure the SPIRIT stuff is all in order so we can get 'em transferred."

The CWSs before her nodded wordlessly while taking notes. There was a knock at the door before it opened—it was Lisa Morales. Before Marie could ask what was up, Lisa spoke, "Just got word," she announced almost breathlessly, "They found Fanny. She's at the hospital!"

"*What?!*" Marie and Kevin shouted in unison.

"Nick just called," Lisa went on, "He's there with his girlfriend…said they brought Fanny in, bandaged up and unconscious."

Marie sat back in her chair and looked upward, as if to say, *Thank You, God!* "Karen and I are gonna head over, see what's goin' on." Lisa concluded.

"You let us know soon as you know something," Marie directed, "Understand?"

"Got it!" Lisa said, and she was gone.

The Local Office boss glanced at the two Case Work Sups before her and thought: *Am I finally seeing the light? Am I nearing the end of the tunnel?*

■ ■

Arlene Rollins returned to the LO and briefed her supervisor on the MVRs. Upon arriving to her desk, she saw the red light on her phone, indicating that someone had called and left her a voicemail message.

The message was not friendly. "This is Miss Peters," said the voice in an edgy tone, "I thought you was gonna come back an' lemme know 'bout my light bill. They done shut ma' lights off an' we got no 'lectricity…"

Arlene now remembered. Peters was the family that she and Paulette went out to see when that body was found in their car. *It was also the last case that Paulette had worked on!*

She attempted to return Ms. Peters' call, to no avail. *The number you have dialed is not in service…*

She began an emergent check request through the LOBA (Local Office Bank Account), but not knowing how much was owed, left the amount blank. Going into Bryan's office, she relayed the voicemail message to him.

"Why don't you run over there, see what's up," he said upon hearing, "See if you can get her bill, bring it here and call PSE&G. Once we find out what the deal is, we can go from there."

Arlene got back in her State car and drove to the Peters' residence in the projects. Parking, she remembered the body. She said a silent prayer that nothing else would go down. She knocked on the apartment door and was met with a hostile mom. "Now you show up?" she asked in a harsh voice, "Where in 'a hell ya been all 'is damn time?"

Arlene started to say something in response, but stopped herself. Doubtful that this woman knew about Paulette, she was *not* about to tell her, either. "Miss Peters," she began, "I'm sorry for what's—"

"*Sorry?*" the angry mom cut her off, "Hell ya mean 'sorry'? Fuckin' PSE&G done shut my damn *lights off!* How the hell ya gonna stan' there an' say you 'sorry'---"

"I need to see your bill, please?" Arlene cut off the other's tirade. With an audible *hmph,* the florid mom went to a table and retrieved the statement. "Here!" she reached it over to the worker.

Arlene took the bill and read it. It was a shut-off notice totaling $403.26. "May I take this, please?" she asked.

"I don' care if ya *eat* it!" Ms. Peters snarled. "The hell I'm gonna do wit' no lights now?"

"Let's see what we can do to get your lights back on, Miss Peters." Arlene said levelly.

Doubtless the woman before her was beyond reasoning; would be a waste of time and effort to try and calm her down. "I tried to call you, but your phone's off. There any other way to contact you?"

The mom told the worker that she had run out of minutes on her phone, but should have more by tomorrow. Arlene stated that she would call the utility company and arrange to get service restored. "Hopefully by tomorrow," she said, "you'll have your lights *and* phone back on." She thanked the mother and left.

Driving back to the office, Arlene thought, *I thanked her, but she never thanked* me!

With the call to PSE&G, she completed the LOBA request. With Bryan's and Kevin's approvals, a check was made out for the arrears; it would require a signature from Marie (or a CWS, in the LO Manager's absence), and once done, remitted to the utility company.

The phone on Arlene's desk rang. "Hello, may I help you?" she greeted the caller.

"Arlene?"

"Yes, this is she."

"This is Frank Hewitt from the Law Guardian's office."

"Yes, Mr. Hewitt, what can I do for you?"

"I understand you went out to see the McEnery family earlier?" inquired Hewitt.

"Yes, I did."

"Did you have some words with the elder daughter?" asked Hewitt.

"No, I didn't."

"Well, apparently," Hewitt said, "she called our office and complained about you. Said that you were rude to her and spoke nasty."

Arlene could not believe what she was hearing. She was nothing but civil and professional—the girl, in fact, was rude to *her!*

"Now, that ain't true!" she spoke in defense, "I was out there, yeah. Fact is, I tried to talk to her. She rolled her eyes and sucked her teeth at me. Matter a' fact, the caregiver got on her about her attitude." Arlene stated to the Law Guardian. "Didn't you at least speak with the caregiver?" she added as an afterthought.

"We're gonna be contacting the caregiver very shortly." said Hewitt, "Just that this young lady called us up and told us that you didn't talk about her and her brother going back home, and how you were supposedly rude to her—"

"I suggest you call the caregiver before you go any further," Arlene cut him off, "And if there's gonna be any more allegations about my attitude or whatever, you need to check it out further before any fingers are pointed!"

"Nobody's pointing any fingers!" Hewitt said testily, "Nobody's accusing anyone of anything. Just wanna hear your side of the story."

"Well, you got my side of it," Arlene

assured the other, "And I know that Mom has court this week also. Hopefully we can get this nonsense resolved by the time we get to court—if not sooner."

After ringing off with Hewitt, she went back to Bryan's office. She told him about the phone call. "Just document it *and* that girl's attitude in your contact form." he advised. "We've been dealing with that family a long time. There's always some shit with them; just do what needs to be done."

Arlene returned to her desk and stared at the case files sitting before her. The Peters case; this other with the obnoxious daughter and druggie Mom; followed by four other caseloads with dysfunctional parents, dysfunctional children…

She had to get away, somehow. But to where?

Her gut had told her that the job would wear her down, but her head had tried to convince her otherwise. First the dead body, then Paulette's suicide, and now a caseload of dysfunctionality—a caseload? Try *several* caseloads! The Law Guardian's call being the icing on the cake. If prayer was the answer, she needed it. A long, strong prayer at that!

But there was something else to ease the burden, other than prayer…

■■

"Fanny, can you hear me?"

Nick was trying to communicate with his colleague. She was semi-conscious and incoherent. IV tubes were attached to her body.

It was all he could say before she was rushed into surgery to repair damages from her gunshot wounds. After Fanny was taken to the Operating Room, he called Karen and informed her, then rushed back to Amy and conveyed the news to her.

"Thank God!" she said, as if relieved of major stress. "She all right?"

"She's in the OR now," said Nick, "They're working to get her better. Question is, are *you* all right?" he looked into his sweetheart's eyes.

"I guess I'm okay," she said, "I just—"

"You *guess?*" Nick asked, looking at her closely.

Amy knew that look. "I'm fine." she assured him.

Nick was not convinced. "You sure?" he asked warily.

"Guess I just had a dizzy spell," she said,

"Side effects from the meds and chemo, I suppose."

They went without speaking for a minute or two, then Amy suggested, "Why don't you go check on your coworker, find out if she's okay."

Nick looked at her. "Go!" she said, "I'll be here, don't worry 'bout me."

"I'll be right back." Nick assured her.

In the waiting area he saw Karen and Lisa. After a brief greeting, he filled the others in on what he saw upon Fanny's arrival. She was in the OR, they had been told, but her condition is serious. While talking, a man came rushing in and hollered at one of the nurses, "My sister was brought here…" he gave Fanny's name.

Nick walked over, "Are you Jason?"

The other affirmed.

Nick introduced himself and the two shook hands. "Your sister's here," he assured, "She's in the OR being treated for a couple wounds." He saw Jason's shoulders drop, as if to say "Thank God!"

Jason was introduced to Karen and Lisa, and all took seats. "It was all over the news," said Jason, "You have no idea how scared shitless I was. Still am. I called our folks in PA," he went on, "They're on their way here now." The three sat quietly and listened as

Jason spoke, "She's just so independent, so…free-spirited. Our mom and dad begged her to come out to PA with 'em. She refused. Preferred to stay where she was—is.

"Never realized how dangerous her job could be," he continued further, "Whoever thought that it would go this far—I mean, for takin' kids away from their mom…"

"Not that it *does* go this far," Lisa cut in, "We can't discuss the situation, you know. Confidentiality and all, but we're sorry for all that's gone down."

Nick suspected that the conversation might turn ugly. That Jason might, just might, look for someone to blame for what had happened to his sister. And probably point the finger at the two supervisors seated before him. As politely as he could, he excused himself. "Be back in a few," he said, "Need to check on Amy." And he was gone.

Amy's eyes were closed when he returned. Thinking that she was asleep, he walked lightly into the room. She opened her eyes upon his sitting beside her. "Thought you were asleep." he said.

She shook her head. "How is she?"

"Still in the OR," he answered. He further told her that Fanny's brother was there, as were Karen and Lisa. "We should know more soon."

Amy and Karen knew each other. They had met at several past job functions—Christmas parties and barbecues. "Karen's here, too?" she asked.

"Uh huh."

"Surprised that Marie and the other bigwigs aren't here." she said, a touch of bitterness in her voice.

He sat, thinking about her last statement. *Do Chiefs mingle with Indians?* Gently, he took her hand in his, pulled it toward himself and kissed lightly.

■■

In an adjacent wing just off from the main hospital, Paul Zahorsky was in recuperation. Speech therapy had begun for him. Sounds emitted from his mouth, but no words.

Aphasia is not uncommon in stroke victims, and those who suffer undergo intense therapy with the hope of regaining the ability to speak.

The therapist was helping Paul form sounds

into words—or rather, syllables—but it was a slow, frustrating process. Frustrating for the patient. About the only decipherable noise he could make were *ehhh* for "yes" and *nnng* for "no".

He was wheelchair bound, but unable to even push himself. His right arm—in fact, his entire right side—was without feeling.

His wife Wendy came every day to help feed him, take him to the bathroom and even clean him up. But she excused herself to tend to their daughter.

Stroke or not, Paul saw the coolness in his wife. No doubt she'd think her husband a burden on the family, and she did not want to deal with caring for a helpless man. She had already been down on him for taking a job she thought "below expectations", and the marriage was already rocky aside from such.

And then there was the rape allegation! Despite the assurance that he would be exonerated, Paul concluded that the real damage had been done to his good name and honest reputation.

And so, he sat quietly with the thoughts of reality weighing him down. He closed his eyes and dozed off with the thoughts of peacefulness.

The peacefulness of sitting in a garden, surrounded by flowers and birds.

The peacefulness of a waterfall, spilling and splashing off a small cliff.

The peacefulness of children playing and laughing, enjoying the day.

It was during this time of peaceful thoughts that an attendant shook him awake, "Mr. Zahorsky," said the staffer, gently nudging him.

No response.

"Mr. Zahorsky," the staffer repeated, shaking him a little harder.

"*Paul!*" the staffer repeated again, louder.

His wrist was grabbed and checked for pulse. There was no pulse to be taken.

Family Service Worker Paul Zahorsky was dead.

****

Arlene had driven past it many a time. In fact, nearly on a daily basis. She knew the location, and the inhabitants within.

She was stressed and overwhelmed. Prayer had helped to a point, but she still needed an "edge" to push her along. She parked her car a couple of blocks from her destination, preferring to walk the remaining distance. Perhaps distance enough for her to gather her thoughts.

Arriving to the front door, she rapped two knocks, followed by one. She knew the code. Someone looked through the peephole and the door opened very slowly. Arlene knew what she wanted—she closed-handedly placed a twenty-dollar bill in the other person's palm and almost immediately—just as stealthily— was given a glassine packet.

Once at home, settled in, she stared at the packet, now laid out on the table before her. *Lord, forgive me!* she thought as she spilled out the packet's contents, and with a scraper blade cut the substance into a folded matchbook.

Taking a deep breath, she lifted the matchbook to her nostril, and sniffed.

It had been some years since Arlene's last trip. Now she was remembering that good contact feeling she experienced, and with it, the pressures and bad feelings of the job, and life, were leaving her body.

∙ ∙

"She's suffered some nerve damage…she has a punctured lung and arterial damage. She also has a bad concussion…"

The Operating Room doctor was advising as to Fanny's condition at present, "…she is expected to recover, but it's going to take time."

Jason, along with Karen and Lisa, felt the relief. "Can I go in and see her?" he asked.

"Yes," said the doctor, "But just you, for now." He looked at the others, "I'm sorry, but only immediate family at this time."

The two supervisors were disappointed, but relieved that their colleague was okay. "We'll head on back to the office," Lisa said, "Give her our love and tell her we'll be back soon."

Nick, at that moment, walked up. "How is she?"

They told him. He also breathed a sigh of relief. "How's Amy?" asked Karen, as an afterthought.

Given all that's happened, Nick had never updated Karen about Amy. One of those *Oh, shit!* Moments. Now, he felt guilty. "She's fine," he said. "She had passed out, but is awake now and alert."

"I'd like to see her, say hello." Karen said.

Nick did not want Karen to see Amy in her condition, yet he couldn't find a reason to say no. "She's just down the hall. C'mon." he said, a touch of reluctance in his voice.

Amy was actually glad to see Karen again; they chatted pleasantly and Amy smiled. Nick introduced Lisa, and the three women talked as if they were old friends.

The two bosses bade their farewells after several minutes, wishing Amy to get well, and in leaving, Nick told them that he would see them tomorrow. After they left, he turned to his lady.

He thought she would be upset, but she was actually cheery and smiled as she looked back at him. "I owe you an apology." he said.

"You owe me nothing."

"I didn't want them to see you this way." he said, regret in his voice.

"Nick, don't worry," she said, taking his hand, "Just a little obstacle in the road of life. We all have 'em."

"They don't know about your condition," he explained, "I never told anyone."

Amy loved that about Nick. He never discussed their personal affairs with anyone; figured that whatever he, Amy, or both were going through was their business and theirs alone. "You can tell Karen." she said to him.

"Why, might I ask?"

"Well," she reasoned, "given the frequent trips to the doctor…the chemo…the meds…side effects, you might need to drop everything and be there for me."

"And you will make a full recovery!" Nick emphasized, looking into her eyes, "You *will* conquer and recover—no ifs, ands, or buts!"

They were silent for a few minutes after. Finally, Amy said, "I'm glad that Fanny's been found alive."

Nick, after a beat or two, said, "So am I."

■■■

Karen and Lisa, upon returning to the LO, were summoned to Marie's office. They briefed the boss on Fanny, mentioning her injuries and expectation to recover.

Marie, listening, sat stonily. She did not smile, nor show any signs of positive look. The two sups noticed this. "What's wrong?" asked Lisa.

"I have some bad news." Marie announced.

"Oh, no!" Karen said, "What now?"

Marie looked at Karen, then at Lisa, "Paul just died."

Lisa was disbelieving, "Are you *friggin' KIDDING ME???!!*"

"I wish more than anything it wasn't true!" Marie answered mournfully.

Lisa still could not believe what she heard. "If this is a cruel joke, I'm not laughin'!"

"No," Marie said, looking levelly at her, "It's *not* a joke, and I'm *not* laughing either!"

Lisa and Karen sat speechlessly. "I'm so sorry, Lisa," said Marie, "Paul was a good guy, I know he was good with the clients, and…"

Lisa could hear no more. Flinging the office door open with a bang, she stormed down the hall toward the door. Several workers, stopping to look, noticed tears flowing down her face as she began to whimper. As she reached the outside, she leaned against a wall and shook as she sobbed uncontrollably.

■ ■

The worker who had called out sick had forgotten to inform of an impending visitation scheduled for that day. And at the time of the scheduled visit, no one had gone out to pick the children up from the resource home at which they were staying. Why? Because no one knew.

Now the biological parents were at the Local Office, in anticipation of their visit with the children—only to discover that the worker was out sick, and left no notification. Thus, the children were a no-show.

"Goddammit, *where're our kids???*" The parents were pounding on the receptionist's window. "You people fuckin' took our kids away, an' now we can't even *see* 'em? *Where the hell's our kids, Goddammit? WHAT THE FUCK KINDA ORGANIZATION YOU GODDAMN PEOPLE RUNNIN' HERE? WHERE THE FUCK'S OUR KIDS???!!??*

The poor receptionist was besieged with these parents screaming at her, the phone ringing, and workers asking about this or that. Now she was trying to get these maniacal parents to calm down. "Wait," she said, "Let me page the worker."

Of course, the worker was not in the office. "Let me get the supervisor," she said, trying to appease the livid couple. This produced no results either—the sup was in court. Now, the parents continued their screaming and cursing tirade.

A Case Work Supervisor was found and summoned to the front lobby. The CWS introduced herself to the parents and calmly asked what the problem was. Still wound up, the parents unloaded on her about their scheduled visit, the kids' not being there and the worker's unavailability. "Okay, all right, please, just calm down," the CWS said in a low, even voice, "We'll find out what's going on, just give us two minutes, please?"

It was discovered that while the assigned worker did call out, the supervisor (not the worker's own) who took the call did not forward the message. That sup would be put on blast and another worker was asked to go out and collect the children to be brought in for their visit.

The visit did take place—forty-five minutes later. The worker who brought the children was asked to supervise the visit. "Who are you?" asked the mother upon the children's arrival to the office.

"I'm the worker assigned to supervise your visit." said the worker. And with that, all settled into one of the visitation rooms.

The children, ages six and three, were active and playful, but at one point the three-year-old stumbled while running and bumped her head. Obviously the child began to cry. "Watch her head there," warned the worker to the parent, "Be careful."

The mother, who along with the father possessed a foul mouth and attitude, said to the worker, "Just sit there and shut up and don't tell me how to watch my kids!"

The worker, not believing what he'd heard, piped up, "Excuse me? What was that you just said?"

"You heard me!" said the mother, looking directly at the worker.

"I will stop this visit right here, right now!" said the worker, "Do *not* talk to me that way…you will—"

"I'll talk to you *any way* I damn well want!" said the mom, her voice rising.

"That's it!" said the worker, "This visit's over. I'm taking the children—"

Now the father got up and got into the worker's face. He began yelling, "Hey, don't you fuckin' *touch* my kids! I'll put you through that wall, motherfucker!"

A supervisor in an adjacent room heard the commotion. She came out and saw the worker and the father standing face-to-face, as if about to come to blows. "Okay, okay, the sup said, moving in between the two, "Sir, you need to calm down," she addressed the father, "You can't be threatening one of our workers."

"*He* can't be threatenin' t' stop our visit!" the enraged parent said, pointing at the worker.

Two other workers, attracted to the noise,

came out to see what was going on. "Call the police," the sup said to one. She turned to the parents, "I'm sorry, but we're gonna have to end your visit—"

"You fuckin' dirty-ass motherfucker—" the father said, and this was followed by a punch to the worker's jaw, knocking him off balance.

The worker, now more than anything, wanted to repay with a punch to the guy's face! But he knew he had to stay professional. *Leave the street attitude on the street!* Regaining his balance, he planted his feet firmly to the floor.

"Are you, all right?" the sup asked him.

His jaw hurt, but still intact, "Yeah, I think so."

Another worker, seeing the incident, moved in quickly and removed the children, who were both crying loudly. The youngsters were taken into another room in which the worker tried to calm them down.

The police arrived almost immediately, and the father was handcuffed and arrested. The mother, screaming obscenities at both the workers and the officers, was also arrested. The worker who was attacked made a report; he was also taken to the hospital to be looked over by a doctor. "If I had that case," the worker told a colleague, "Those people would *never* get those kids back! Not with *that* attitude!"

Little did the worker realize that a TPR—Termination of Parental Rights—was actually being considered for the parents in question, due to founded reports of constant neglect and substance abuse!

■ ■

Nick had mixed feelings upon arriving home from the hospital—good, fair, and poor, in that order.

Amy was doing much better; she was awake, alert, and her meds had been adjusted to deal with her affliction. A couple days' rest and she should be back home, good as new (so it is hoped).

Fanny, while not completely out of danger, was somewhat stabilized. Given the blood loss and punctured lung, among other factors, she would have a long road to recovery.

And it was while en route home that Nick got the dreaded phone call about his friend and colleague, Paul. Karen had called and informed him, for Lisa was too distraught to speak. After hanging up, he pulled over and stopped the car. Given the moisture in his eyes, he was vaguely aware of the tears flowing over and running down his face. *Damn it, Paul…it's hit you too! I'm so, so sorry, man!*

Wiping his face with his hand, and barely conscious of the route traveled, Nick pulled back onto the road and drove directly home.

Home, to an empty house. He just wanted to shut the world out. No more phone calls, no TV, no music, no *nothing!* Throwing his jacket and keys into a chair, he plopped down heavily on the couch and without taking off his sneakers, propped his feet up against the arm of the couch.

Overwhelmed with exhaustion, and he knew it! Nick was tired—physically, mentally, emotionally. Tired of the bullshit, tired of seeing people suffer, tired of the thanklessness…he had vowed that he would not let it get to him, but it was engulfing him like the arms of an octopus.

Silence. It surrounded him, and with it, his ability to think, and think deeply.

He thought of the job. In spite of his long-ago decision to never bring it home at night, he could not help but to think of some of the families he'd dealt with in his career, all of whom had issues—some worse than others.

Nevertheless, he'd made it this far with his integrity still intact. Tattered in a few places, yet still essentially intact.

Colleagues and bosses—many were dedicated, hard workers; others not so dedicated. Nick had seen the hypocrisy, the "prima donnas", the *it's-not-my-job* types with their noses in the air, more than his share of "college-educated-but-no-common-sense" people who, just because they have a title, think that they're the "best thing since the wheel was invented"!

And while on the topic of colleagues, those who had let the job eat them up, inside and out. Some of his coworkers were like minnows in a pool of sharks. If the bosses didn't eat them alive, the families would!

Nick had seen it firsthand. Workers running from the office in tears. Workers cursing. Workers screaming. In one case, a worker and supervisor in a face-to-face confrontation, nearly coming to blows.

The job was a pressure cooker, this could be believed.

Ask Paulette.

Ask Fanny.

Ask Paul.

Work aside, he thought of Amy, and what

she was going through at the moment. He needed someone to talk to, but had no idea who to turn to. His own parents were deceased, and he had one sibling, a sister, who lived in Virginia. He and his sister were never very close, but they did keep in sporadic contact.

He thought of prayer. While not deeply religious, Nick did believe in God. He was once asked about his denomination, and he said he was an "elapsed Catholic". Given the controversies of recent years in the Catholic church, Nick had had second thoughts about Catholicism. For a very brief time, he considered atheism; his rationale being: *If there is a God, why does He allow all these things to happen to people?*

But he soon realized: *God doesn't write our scripts—we write our own! Thus, bad things befall us!*

Not to say that his colleagues, or even Amy, were responsible for their own fall; chalk it up to just plain hard luck! Hard luck, sometimes, is a test of one's strength.

A test of strength…gotta stay strong…gotta keep fightin' the good fight… and with that thought, Nick felt his body relax. From the soles of his feet upward, his body and mind cleared of all depressing thoughts, and relaxed.

****

Arlene Rollins was also in a relaxed state. Her TV on and tuned to the news, she sat staring blankly at the screen.

It did not register in her mind that the news story being shown was that of the missing worker from her own office who had been found—seriously injured but alive. Or that the worker's captors were caught after a high-speed police chase resulting in one dead, another in custody. Arlene was in her own blank world, free from emotion.

Her landline phone rang, it seemed, endlessly. Arlene hardly cared. Her cell phone went off just as many times. Callers began to wonder about her, for she was not picking up any of her calls. Her boyfriend had tried several times to reach out to her, to no avail.

After calling the LO to check on her, he was told that Arlene was gone for the day. Gut instinct telling him that something was wrong, the boyfriend drove to her house. Seeing her car outside, he felt somewhat relieved, yet still felt he should check on her.

He had a key to Arlene's apartment, but out of sheer courtesy, knocked on her door and yelled to her, "Arlene," he announced, "Open the door, it's me!"

No answer.

He pounded on the door, "Arlene!" he shouted, "It's me. open the door!" He could hear the TV playing from within. There was still no response.

"Arlene, I know you're in there," he said, "Open the door, please!"

He was very hesitant to unlock the door and let himself in. Discretion being the better part of valor, he drew his cell phone and punched in 911. He told the operator that he thought something was wrong and could somebody come out to the address?

Three minutes later a police car pulled up. The boyfriend identified himself to the officer and they went to Arlene's door. "Arlene," said the cop, knocking on her door, "It's the police. Open your door, please."

This went on for a few more minutes. By now, another patrol car had arrived and this second officer walked to where the others were.

A small group of people had gathered about thirty yards away. Onlookers.

The first officer turned to the boyfriend and nodded his approval for him to use the key.

The door was opened and the officers entered, instructing the boyfriend to wait by the door. He got upset when he saw one of the cops draw his gun, but said nothing.

Arlene was found sprawled across her couch, her eyes open, staring blankly and catatonic. The first cop grabbed her and shook her as if to wake her, "Arlene," he said, "Wake up. You all right?"

The faded traces of white residue on the table were not unnoticed as the cop tried to shake the woman back to reality. The other officer was searching the apartment room to room while an ambulance was dispatched. The boyfriend, leaning against the doorjamb, looked on. When one of the cops looked his way, he shook his head disbelievingly.

"We got an ambulance comin'," said the cop, "And I'm afraid to tell ya, after she's released from the hospital she's probably gonna go to jail for possession of controlled substance."

This can't be happening! No way! Her boyfriend knew about Arlene's past, but she had put all the bad shit behind her and was moving forward. *This cannot be happening!*

A collection was taken to help pay for Paul Zahorsky's funeral. Cards of condolences and flowers were delivered to his wife and daughter.

Among those who attended the services were Case Work Supervisor Annette Martinez, Unit Sups Karen Emory and Lisa Morales, and several others from the LO.

Nick was there also. He had brought Amy along at her insistence that she also attend. "I'm not fragile," she told him firmly, "I may not have known him as well as you did, but he was your friend and I wanna pay my respects!" He knew better than to argue.

Seeing his friend's body laid out in the casket, Nick thought of the last words he had said to Paul prior to his illness: *Stay away from this place…you're not missing anything!* Nick had to blink a couple of times to keep the tears from flowing. Amy, missing nothing, took his hand and held it in hers as they sauntered away from the bier. Nick, releasing Amy's hand momentarily, took Wendy Zahorsky's hand and gave a friendly kiss and offer of condolences, repeating the gesture for their daughter.

Paul's daughter, it was noticed, was red-faced, as if she had very recently been crying up a storm. After another minute or two of small talk, Nick conveyed his best and he and

Amy left.

In the car, Amy sat in thought as they drove along. "Can I ask you a question?" she piped up, breaking the silence.

"Of course." *Uh oh, here it comes!*

"When I called you the other day," she began, "why didn't you tell me about Paul?"

It was the day that he collapsed on the couch. He had gotten home from the hospital, and weighed down with stress, fell asleep without realizing it. Amy's call had awakened him.

"You know, Amy," he stated, "To tell you the truth, there are a bunch of reasons." He looked at her briefly.

"I'm listening." she said, paying full attention.

"One, I was keeping into consideration your condition at the time. Your passing out really scared the shit out of me; I wanted to make sure you had the best of care."

"And two?" she asked.

"Two, just as I—*we*—" he made sure to install *we* instead of *I*, "were getting your information together, they brought Fanny in. Remember I said that I called when I realized who it was."

Amy considered this. It wasn't unreasonable. "And given all the talk about Fanny and me, I guess it could have been overlooked." she concluded.

"That's not all." Nick added.

Amy looked curiously at him. "Nobody knew at the time!" he concluded.

"So, even when I called you—"

"When you called me," he nodded, "I knew. Got the news on my way home, but didn't want to overwhelm you." He looked at her again. "Guess the reason I didn't tell you was…well…you got enough on your plate as is…"

"Nick, how many times I gotta tell you," Amy said, "what affects you, affects me too?"

"I know that, but—"

"But, *nothing!*" Amy was vehement, "I love you, and I worry about you! I understand your concern about me, but dammit, anything you've got on your mind, good or bad, *let me in* on it! I may not be able to do much, but at least let me be your sounding board, will ya?"

Nick was quiet. You couldn't win with Amy. "Okay, I get the message. I got it." he said after several seconds of silence.

"Promise me." she said, still looking his way.

"Promise." he said in a low voice.

They stopped for a red light. "Look at me and *promise* me!" she insisted.

"Honey, I gotta drive," he said, "I can't look at you, I gotta watch the road." A sly smirk played on his face.

"We're stopped at a light." she said. She knew his trick. "Now look at me. And *promise me!*"

He turned and looked straight into her eyes. "Okay, I promise." he said.

"Thank you."

"You're welcome." He turned to look at the road as the light turned green. Her eyes were on his mind now. "Incidentally," he said, "How're you feeling today?"

"With my hands." she answered. They both laughed.

"I meant," he said as the laughter died down, "You feel okay? Any nausea, pain, weakness or anything?"

"Why?" she asked. Amy was like a detective.

"Nothing. Just asking."

"What's on your mind, Nick Donovan?" He knew he was not going to be let off the hook when she mentioned his first *and* last name.

He gave her a look again. She caught it. "Maybe," she said, "If you're a good boy, then just *maaayyybeeee…*"

Fanny Palumbo was awake.

She blinked several times and discovered that it hurt to even turn her head. Moving only her eyes, she noticed the IV tubes, the bandages, the blood pressure and pulse-monitoring machine and institutional drop ceiling with fluorescent lights above her head.

Now a nurse was in the room with her. The nurse was adjusting the tubes and monitoring the digital machine readings. Fanny wanted to speak, but in doing so her voice came out but an octave or two above a whisper. "What's going on?" she tried to say.

The nurse, seeing that she was now awake, went to her, "Hey, you're awake!" she said in a light, upbeat voice, "You're okay, honey. Everything's fine. You're a little banged up, but you're gonna be all right. Can I get you anything?"

Fanny's mouth was dry, but still she tried to speak.

"You're in the hospital, sweetie," the nurse informed her, "You're gettin' the best of care. No need to worry. Want I should get the doctor?"

Fanny nodded slightly and rasped a "Yes".

"Just relax, sweetie," said the nurse, "You went through a rough time, but the doc'll talk to you. Hang on, lemme get him. Be back in a minute." She left the room.

Fanny knew that she did go through a rough time, but *how* rough? It was coming back to her; she last remembered that Mrs. DiCiccio had pointed that gun at her! Did the gun go off? Was she shot? Did that crazy bitch crash the car they were riding in? *What the hell happened?*

The nurse returned shortly with the doctor in tow. "Hello there," he spoke, "I'm Dr. Solberg. Understand you just woke up." Fanny looked up at the doctor, a robust man with a salt-and-pepper goatee and piercing blue eyes.

She wanted a drink of water. Reading this, the nurse extracted a small plastic cup, poured some water from a pitcher, and gently put the cup to Fanny's mouth. She consumed the liquid in small gulps, droplets spilling from the sides of her mouth and down her chest and arm. The cup was pulled away and while Fanny gently licked her lips, the nurse wiped her mouth and chin. Finding some more of her voice, she asked slowly, weakly, "What's going on?"

"Well," said Dr. Solberg, exhaling, "For one thing, you have a couple gunshot wounds. You also have a small concussion, seems you've been tossed around a bit." The doctor spoke slowly, "Along with the concussion, you have a couple broken ribs, a punctured lung, most likely from a gunshot wound; you've also sustained a second gunshot wound to your left shoulder. You've suffered a bit of bleeding, obviously—internally and externally. We've removed the round that's hit you…I say 'round', because apparently, the other exited your body. Patched you up as well as we could.

"We're sure you're gonna be fine, but for now, you're gonna need to be on IV support. Your vitals are fine, but I'm afraid you'll be in some discomfort for a time. This means you'll be out of circulation—at least, until you heal."

Fanny looked away briefly, trying to absorb this piece of information. At least she was alive, and that was what counted!

"Your brother and parents are waiting just outside," the doctor announced, "You up to seeing 'em?"

She nodded.

"Okay," smiled Dr. Solberg, "So just rest up, get better. I'll send your family in." he concluded, and left the room.

Even in her semi-coherence, Fanny had a feeling that the doctor was keeping something from her. However, she decided to just "rest up and get better", as the doctor advised.

Her parents walked in, along with her brother. Mrs. Palumbo bore an almost striking resemblance to her daughter, but was an inch shorter and about twenty pounds heavier. "Are you all right, honey?" she began to cry as she rushed to Fanny's side.

"I…think so." was the answer. Fanny tried to smile as she looked at her mom.

Mrs. Palumbo took her daughter's hand in her own, but Fanny noticed that she had had little feeling in her left hand. She said nothing about it. All spoke for several minutes, happy that she was awake and alert—and alive! Some awkward silence followed their talking. "What's wrong?" Fanny asked, looking first at her mom, then her dad, and then Jason.

Mr. Palumbo cleared his throat slightly. He was a man of medium height with a stocky build. "Honey," he began, "We want you to come home with us. You've been through so much here, and—"

"Dad," said Fanny, "I know you guys're worried about me. but I'm fine. I'll be fine. Worse things have—"

"That's what we're afraid of," said her dad, "*Worse* things."

"Do we really need to discuss this now?" asked Fanny, "I mean, *really?*"

"All right, okay," said her mom, trying to smooth it over, "We'll drop it." She looked at her husband.

"Where're you staying?" Fanny asked, "Or are you headed back home?"

"At your brother's." said her mom, glancing in Jason's direction.

Fanny looked at one, then the other, with her eyes. She still could not move her head without a world of searing pain. After several more minutes, her parents announced that they were going to go, but will see her tomorrow. "I want you should rest up, understand?" Mrs. Palumbo ordered, kissing her daughter on the head.

"Yes, Mother." Fanny answered mockingly.

"We'll see you tomorrow," said her dad, "Love you."

"Love you too." said Fanny.

As the parents were leaving, Jason lagged behind. "Go on," he called out to them, "I'll be with you in a minute." He turned to his sister. Something was wrong; she knew the look.

"Did the doc talk to you?" he asked.

"Talk to me about what?" she was looking at him now.

He glanced toward the door, then looked back at her, "That shot you took to your shoulder…shattered the bones severely. Also tore up some tissue and nerves…"

"And?" she looked at him intensely.

He sighed before continuing, "He said the nerves in your shoulder and upper arm are so badly damaged…that you may have permanent loss of use or feeling in your left arm."

This was more than Fanny could take in one sitting. "Oh, shit!" she said, not believing it to be true. "Oh, shit! *Shit! Shit!*" and the tears flowed like a river.

■·

Arlene had come to, and was feeling lightheaded and dizzy.

It took her a few seconds to realize that she was not on her couch, but on a stretcher. In a strange room with very bright lighting. A hospital room.

It took her a few more seconds to realize further that she was secured to the stretcher; a set of handcuffs securing her wrist to the side railing.

She had no idea how she'd gotten here—she had no idea *when* she'd gotten here. In fact, she had no idea what had even happened!

A nurse came in to check on her. "How y' feelin'?" she asked in greeting.

Arlene looked at the nurse blankly, "What

happened?" she asked.

"Apparently," the nurse answered carefully, "you ingested some dangerous substance."

It was slowly coming back. What she had taken, where she had gotten what she had taken…but she remembered no more afterward.

"Seems that your boyfriend found you," the nurse went on, "911 was called and you were brought here."

Arlene looked at her cuffed wrist. "What's with these cuffs?" she asked.

The nurse's tone had changed. "I understand that you are under police guard," she said in a not-as-friendly tone, "There's a police officer outside the door there; you need to speak with him and get the information." The nurse finished her duties and left the room.

Arlene looked astonished after the nurse as she departed. A few seconds later, a big, ruddy-faced cop walked in.

"What's going on, officer?" asked Arlene curiously.

The officer looked at the woman through narrow eyes, "Miss," he began, "You're being placed under arrest for possession of controlled dangerous substance. We found traces of cocaine on your table."

Arlene, not believing what she was hearing, wanted to ask how the police had gotten into her house. Instinct told her not to ask.

"At this time, I must advise you of your rights…" and the cop went on with the Miranda just as it is heard on every TV cop show. When asked if she understood her rights, Arlene nodded slowly, looking downward. Her eyes became wet, and within a second, tears raced down her cheeks.

"Once you're released from here," the cop went on, "we'll be taking you for booking and processing." He stood there for a few more seconds and then left the room.

It was all Arlene could take. She had had a relapse, and now because of it, she's lost her freedom, her dignity, and quite possibly, her job and career! All for one fast high to get her mind at ease! *All pain, no gain!*

Nick felt as if he were doing the work of five people. He *was* doing the work of five people! He had to monitor his own scheduled client transports and visits; he was also doing some of Paul's assignments. There was curiosity as to who would take over Fanny's assignments as well.

Add to this, of course, he had been monitoring Amy's progress while she was on her meds; she had gone through treatments, and so far, so good—the only side effects being the nausea and vomiting. It didn't help matters that Fanny was in the same hospital Amy had been.

Now with Amy back home and resting, Nick felt that he could concentrate on his work. He called frequently to check on her until she assured him repeatedly that she was fine. Amy Paladino was a self-sufficient woman.

"Where's Paul?" the question was asked directly upon arrival to the resource home Nick had gone to. Paul had been the primary transporting and monitoring worker of this scheduled visitation; the caregiver and children within the home liked and respected him.

Nick hated lying. He firmly believed that you got further by telling the truth. But he could not bring himself to tell about his coworker's fate. "Paul…couldn't be here today." he said.

It was the same upon arrival to the office. The two children Nick transported were having a supervised visit with their biological mom. The mother was also inquisitive about Paul.

The visit otherwise went well, the children interacted with their mom and afterward, Nick returned the youngsters to their resource home.

Exiting the vehicle to escort the kids inside, Nick warmly greeted the caregiver, a plump woman in her early fifties with a warm smile and demeanor. "We hadn't officially met when I got here to pick the kids up," he said, extending his hand, "Nick Donovan."

"Audrey Silver," the caregiver said, shaking Nick's hand, "How are ya?"

"Do you have a few minutes to spare?" Nick asked, "I know you're busy and I'll try not—"

"Oh, sure, sure," said Ms. Silver, "Come in. Can I get ya anything? Coffee or something?"

"No, thank you." Nick said politely. He faced the caregiver and his expression grew serious. The other read this and immediately knew that something was wrong. "Did the kids misbehave?" she asked, "Did they give you a hard time?"

"No, nothing like that at all," said Nick, "In fact, they were well-behaved and the visit was great." She looked at him with full attention as he spoke, "Ms. Silver," he began.

"Call me Audrey, please." she said.

Lisa had asked Nick to inform the caregiver about Paul. "I'm afraid I have some bad news to deliver…" he began, and told her about Paul's passing.

"Oh, no!" she said, still looking at Nick, "Oh, *nooo*…"

The worker had to blink to keep the tears from spilling over. He still hurt in thinking about his friend and colleague.

"Mr. Donovan…" she began.

"Nick," he insisted, and as he did so, he saw her tears flow.

"Paul is such a good man…" she said, "Such a sweet, gentle person. Those kids love him; they look forward to him picking them up for their visit…"

Nick had noticed that the caregiver refrained from referring to Paul in the past tense. Delayed reaction, perhaps. "I am very sorry," she said, taking his hand, "I don't know how I'm gonna tell the kids." She wiped a tear away. "They're gonna be crushed…we're gonna miss him so much…"

I miss him so much already! thought Nick. Outwardly, he said, "I am so very sorry." His hand still in hers, he placed the other hand atop the two, looked at Ms. Silver and softly spoke the words, "Say a prayer." Releasing his hands, he turned and exited the house.

As he climbed back into the minivan and

started the engine, the tears began to flow, yet again.

■ ■

Fanny was in a trance. She knew that she was in bad shape, but this latest information was more than she could bear.

Punctured lung…nerve damage…shattered bones…and now, possible paralysis in her arm! Why didn't that crazy bitch just *kill* her and get it over with?

That she was in immeasurable pain—despite being doped up with heavy medication—was one thing. But the inability to use her left arm put her in an emotional black hole.

She lay staring, unblinkingly, at the ceiling, the IV functioning, the machines beeping. How could she possibly function? she thought. Taken for granted the things she did every day: writing, cooking a meal, driving a car, planting…there was no way that Fanny could again do the things she enjoyed most—not with a bum arm!

Loss of ability, loss of independence. Now, she feared, she'd *have* to have someone care for her and do things for her. Fanny was an independent woman, and prided herself on such!

Those days, in her viewpoint, were over, and Fanny fell into an emotional abyss.

Meanwhile, two detectives were speaking with her parents and brother, trying to gather information. Unbeknownst to her parents, Fanny's kidnapping had made the news. Thus, they were quite surprised when reporters showed up at Jason's door. When the Palumbos discovered *who* had actually kidnaped and hurt their daughter, it became an insistence: Fanny will *not* live in New Jersey any longer—she will live in Pennsylvania, where her parents will look after her!

"Good luck tellin' her that!" Jason had told the folks, but he knew also that his sister had no choice. Disability retirement will help some, but the doctor visits, therapy, outpatient treatments and such will take a lot of her (and their) time.

"I am *not* letting my daughter stay here with those…*hoodlums!*" Mrs. Palumbo spoke out, "I'll be damned if I'm gonna let those lowlifes get her again!" She was not one to be intimidated; even the detectives read this.

"Has your daughter ever complained to you

about her job?" one of the detective asked.

"There's always something to complain about," said Mrs. Palumbo laconically, "What do you think? Look at the kinda people she's gotta deal with…"

"Did she say or mention anyone in particular?"

"No." was the answer, "And even if she did, who gives a shit? Far's I'm concerned, they're all no damn good!"

It was determined that the detectives would not get any information from Fanny's parents—the Pope could be a lowlife in their opinion!

Back at the hospital the next day, they tried to engage their daughter in light conversation, to little avail. She lay unfocused, staring, existing yet saying not more than one- or two-word responses. Her body and mind closed off to all…

■■

Arlene was in a wheelchair, handcuffed.
She was being released from the hospital.
The attending doctor, prescription shown to

the arresting officer prior to being given to Arlene, had given the OK to release.

An attendant flanked by two officers was wheeling her to the exit door. "We'll take 'er from here." one of the officers barked as they reached the door. Arlene's wrists were cuffed in front and both cops lifted her from the chair and walked her to the police car. One of the officers opened the rear door and she was placed in the backseat.

As the car drove off, Arlene sat quietly staring out the windshield through the prisoner's cage. She had ruined herself, she thought. Lost her job, her career, everything. Was it worth it? *Was it really worth it?*

The car pulled into the police station parking area and when it stopped, the passenger officer got out, opened the back door, and Arlene climbed out wordlessly. The officer took her by the upper arm and led her into a back door of the station.

Inside, one of her wrists was uncuffed as she was led to a bench and instructed to sit. Upon doing so, her wrist was recuffed to a steel bar attached to the wall. The officer then went inside a room to process the paperwork; his partner joined him a few minutes later.

The first officer, after about twenty minutes, came back out and asked Arlene if she wanted to call anyone. Arlene said no, her boyfriend had already known that the police were arresting her; hopefully he'd get bail money—or find someone who will. And a lawyer at that.

Removing the handcuffs, the officer took her into a back room, in which she was processed—searched thoroughly (by a female officer), fingerprints, mug shot—and placed into a holding cell. "You'll be seein' the judge in just a little while," said the officer, "So just hang tight 'til somebody comes to get ya."

Arlene didn't know whether to take the cop's remark as sincerity or sarcasm.

Sitting on the cold, hard cell bunk, she tried to recall everything that had gone down leading to her being locked up. Arlene knew that she had let things get to her; she had been doing fine lately. But then so much of so much—the body in the car, Paulette's death, the overwork, the pain and suffering…and then, her relapse. *Who, What, Where, When, Why,* and the most essential, *How.*

LO Manager Marie Kovacs had had enough on her plate. More than enough.

Given all the goings-on within her command, it seemed that her workers and supervisors were running around as if the world were ending in five minutes! The cases were piling up, the paper was not nearly caught up, and the court reviews…forget it! The judge was not a happy camper of late.

Add to this, her own boss, Area Director Kathy Blasi was calling frequently—a little *too* frequently—to ask questions regarding this case or that.

Her way of telling me to get my ass in gear, thought Marie.

In addition, to top the icing on the cake, her own marriage was on the rocks. Twelve years and four children after the blissful vows, she and her husband were estranged—living together for the sake of the kids, but perfect strangers under the same roof.

A mound of paperwork on her desk, Marie knew the contents therein. A couple of complaints from parents, mixed in with Fanny's medical condition, as well as grief counseling literature, as the workers who died were still being mourned. And the information anew concerning the hospitalization and subsequent arrest of Arlene.

Studying herself in the mirror that morning

while applying light makeup, Marie noticed the strands of gray in her brown hair. Upon her appointment as LO Manager a few years ago, she had had maybe one or two small strands of gray; now she had seven or eight times as much.

There was a light rap on her office door, which was ajar. She looked up in time to see Kevin Beck stroll in. "Got a sec?" he asked.

"What's up?"

"Spoke with the arresting officer," he began in a low voice, as he shut the door for privacy, "Apparently Arlene had a faded line of coke on her table when she was found. ER report says that she had gotten some 'bad coke' that put her out.

"She was taken in after the hospital released her," Kevin went on, "Her boyfriend just bailed her out about an hour ago. Tried calling her house, and her cell. No answer, so I guess she's with him."

"You know that a report's gotta be done, right?" Marie spoke directly. More of a command than a question.

The Manager and the Case Work Sup looked at each other. The response was unspoken. "Do what needs to be done." she said, turning her attention back to her papers.

Kevin hated this part of the job. That a worker had a substance abuse problem was one thing. In his years on the job, he had seen workers with definite drug- and alcohol-related issues. But for a worker to be arrested and jailed—in other words, caught with their pants down—was yet another factor.

He also knew that given her good work record, Arlene would probably not be removed. The Division, as well as the court, would order her to attend a substance-abuse rehabilitation program. Her arrest may leave a black mark in her personnel file, may even impede her chances of future promotion. However, she will in some likelihood keep her job with the Division—worst case scenario, get reassigned to another office.

Kevin's cell phone went off and he answered it. "Yeah?" he said busily.

"Kevin, it's Arlene."

"Yea, Arlene, how's it goin'?"

"Guess you heard."

"You guessed right."

"Oh." she said, the dejection not unnoticeable.

"You okay?" he asked, to make conversation.

"Yea, I'm okay." she said, sighing. There was some silence that followed, and then she asked, "What happens now?"

Kevin sighed audibly, then said, "Well, we don't know what happens, but a report's been made to HQ. As of now, you're on suspension pending further notice."

Arlene responded with a sigh of her own, "Guess I fucked up big time."

"I don't know what action's gonna be taken from here," Kevin said firmly, "But if I were you, I'd not say anything further 'til speaking with your Union rep."

"Okay," she said in a defeated tone, "I'll call."

"Good luck." he said, and broke the connection.

Arlene hung up, and as she did so collapsed in her boyfriend's arms. She had a tough fight ahead of her, and she knew it. Union…lawyer…court…rehab. She was, she felt, in the fight of her life.

■■■

"Delayed shock."

The doctors were speaking with Fanny's parents and brother. She had become incoherent, staring into space, almost unresponsive.

"She will need intensive therapy." said Dr. Solberg, "Not just physical, but emotional."

The Palumbos knew it all too well. That one would be reduced to a near-helpless state after so many years of independence could be devastating, most especially to the victim of affliction.

There was no question or doubt in the decision: *Fanny will live with and be cared for by her parents!* "We will get her only the best therapy there is!" Mrs. Palumbo exclaimed emphatically.

They looked in on their daughter. Fanny was only slightly more responsive, yet noticeably lacked the bubbly happy-go-lucky attitude she was known for. It was also not unnoticed that the heavy medication was taking its toll, making her seem weighed down.

"We're going to have to keep her here for a few more days for observation," said Dr. Solberg, "But I suggest you make outpatient therapy arrangements as soon as possible."

Mr. Palumbo, using his connections, had contacted some places and the arrangements were set. "It's all done," he told the doctor, "They're just waitin' for her arrival."

Meanwhile, Fanny's mom and brother were inside the room, holding her hand and speaking gently. Mr. Palumbo and the doctor shook hands. "Many thanks, Doctor." he said. He then joined the others in the room.

Fanny was smiling slightly and engaged in stilted conversation. A huge bouquet of flowers had arrived, with a card attached. Mrs. Palumbo, reaching for it, looked at the card and then passed it to her daughter. The card contained get-well wishes and signatures from every worker in the Local Office.

"Gotta find some way to thank 'em," Fanny said weakly.

"You will," said her mom. "But for right now, find a way to get better." And for some reason, Fanny was overcome with a feeling that she had not felt in years: the feeling of a contented baby in its mother's arms—loved, nurtured, and not a care in the world!

■■■

Nick had checked in with Karen and then with Lisa, to update both on the latest concerning the most recent visit. He had told about conveying to the caregiver the news about Paul.

"Mrs. Silver was in tears," he said mournfully, "I had to get out of there; I felt myself beginning to lose it. I just didn't wanna be there when she told those kids…"

Lisa gave him a sympathetic look. "You okay, hon?" she asked gently.

Nick was a bit surprised at Lisa's term of endearment, but said, "Yeah, I'm good."

"Go on home," she said, "See ya tomorrow."

He was walking out of the office when Lisa shouted, "Nick?" He turned, looked at her, "Thank you." she said, and there was meaning in her tone.

"You bet." he said, and left.

He called Amy while in transit, informing that he was on his way. He asked how she was—for the umpteenth time, no doubt—and she told him for just as many times that she was fine. She had been to the doctor that day for another checkup, and was still taking her meds.

Arriving home, he showered and donned a sweat suit—his favorite clothing. Amy cooked and served dinner and they ate, light here-and-there conversation between them.

Dinner finished, Nick washed the dishes while Amy watched television. The phone rang and Amy answered it, greeting the caller. After some vague conversation, she said goodbye and hung up. Nick asked with his eyes.

"That was the doctor," she answered his gaze, "She wants to see me in her office tomorrow."

"Everything okay?" he asked, a touch of concern in his voice.

"I don't know," she answered, "She just said she wants to see me tomorrow. Didn't say why."

Much as they tried not to worry, theirs was one sleepless night.

■■■

Arlene had consulted with a representative from the Union.

The Union rep had taken her written claim, and met with Employee Relations, while Arlene contacted an attorney and arranged to enter an in-patient rehabilitation program.

In time, she felt that she was making strides to move forward. Frequent contacts with her Union rep and attorney as well as progress in rehab were making Arlene feel like her old self again.

It also didn't hurt that a worker from the LO kept in contact with her, keeping Arlene informed with the latest shop talk and encouragement to stay strong and continue on.

Arlene had met with a psychologist one day, in the second week of her rehab. She was distrustful of people within, and kept to herself—not one to reveal her business. At first she had cursed the psychologist out and called her a few choice names, but given some time and a few words from the rehab center administrator, Arlene responded— albeit coldly—to the psychologist's requests to meet.

The ice, over time, began to drip and thaw, from coldness to coolness. Before she even realized it, even the cool reception was leaving and some warmness set in its place.

The psychologist had secured Arlene's trust, and ever-so-slowly, she opened up and spoke about her life, her experiences, her career. At one point in her continuing sessions, the emotions overcame her and she sobbed uncontrollably as she spoke of the loss of her friend and colleague Paulette, and the subsequent stresses of her job leading to her relapse, and the arrest that followed.

The psychologist listened attentively, taking

in every word, asking questions and giving small steps of advice to help Arlene in her forward progress.

And Arlene was making some satisfactory strides. Sitting outside one sunny day, she thought deeply of the long road traveled, from gangbanger to youth counselor to college student to CPS worker. With some time for church to study the word of God.

Her attorney had met with the rehab administrator as well. It was determined that Arlene was making good progress and understood her mistakes. Her pastor had also visited her, and together they read and studied verses from the Bible and prayed, asking God to continue to lend His hand in keeping Arlene on the road to recovery. "Just remember," warned her pastor, "He helps those who—"

"Help themselves!" Arlene finished.

∎∎

On a day that the sun was bright in the sky,

Fanny Palumbo was discharged from the hospital.

Her parents arrived to pick her up, and, propped in a wheelchair, she was wheeled through a set of corridors to an elevator. They boarded the down car, went through another corridor, and out to a late-model minivan.

Using her good arm, Fanny got up slowly from the chair and, with her mom's help, climbed into the front passenger seat of the vehicle, her mom insisting on sitting in the center seat behind her.

She still felt pain and discomfort, but not as severely. She also had a long road ahead of her in terms of recovery, and she knew it. She would need close assistance and monitoring, but at least she was alive.

Mr. Palumbo climbed in behind the wheel and started the engine. As he did so he looked at his "little girl" as he considered her, "You okay, sweetie?" he asked.

"Yeah, I'm okay." she said, forcing a slight smile. She was still feeling depressed.

Seat belts fastened, they moved off and away from the hospital. Staring out the window, Fanny tried to think good thoughts, anything *not* to be reminded of how she had gotten where she was. She was not paying attention to the route when the minivan stopped in front of a building. Returning to reality, she instantly knew where she was. "Why are we here?" she asked guardedly.

"Oh," said her mom, "Somebody just wants to see you for a sec."

"No!" Fanny begged, "Please! Not the way I am…"

"You're fine." said her parents as they helped her out of the vehicle. Fanny protested endlessly as she stepped out, went slowly up the walkway and into the building.

She was still protesting when a door opened and everyone screamed: *"SURPRIIIIISE!!!"*

She looked around and there were balloons, ribbons, gifts and a huge cake, atop which were the words: *WELCOME HOME, FANNY!* All of her colleagues standing and applauding amid the loudest ovation she ever heard.

So touched was the worker that she was overcome with tearful emotion.

****

The sleepless night became an irritable morning.

Nick and Amy barely spoke over their morning coffee. Even if they did so, their words were vague and sharp-edged.

Knowing that nothing further could be accomplished by sitting, Nick left for work. At his desk, he kept busy with several contact reports. He picked up the phone on his desk and reached out to a couple of resource parents to arrange scheduled visitations, informing the parties that the biological parents had confirmed their times—and that he, Nick, would be there at the scheduled times to pick the children up for their respective visits.

Calls completed and nearly finishing his reports, his phone rang. It was Karen. "Can you run and pick up Miss Collins," she asked, "Bring her in for a urine screen?" He agreed to do so.

Nick drove out to the residence. Miss Collins, a single mom who had had her child removed a month prior, was known for her substance abuse history. He knocked on the door and a man answered. Apparently, this man was Miss Collins' current boyfriend—or, to be more precise, her bed partner, as she was known to sleep with several different men.

"Miss Collins in?" asked Nick.

The man, a disheveled-looking guy with tattoos on his arms and upper torso, gave the worker the once-over, then grunted something unintelligible. He waddled back inside, leaving the door ajar. Nick heard him say, "Some guy lookin' fer y' at the door."

Nick heard the patter of bare feet and Miss Collins appeared. She was a world-weary-looking woman with brown hair streaked with blonde worn in a ponytail, a strand or two of which hung over her forehead. She was wearing a stained maroon blouse, and as Nick could tell, no bra. She was pushing the hanging strands of hair out of her face as she greeted him. "Yes?" she said.

"Hi, Miss Collins," Nick said, identifying himself, "I'm here to pick you up."

"Pick me up?" she asked quizzically, "For what, may I ask?"

"I'm bringing you to the office for screening."

The woman stood staring at the worker, her mouth open, "I'm sorry," she said, "I can't go. I have a job interview this afternoon at—"

"Did you let someone know of this?" Nick cut her off, "Did you tell my supervisor or another worker that you had an interview?"

"Yes, I…did tell them," she stammered, "I called before and told them that I—"

"Who did you speak with?" asked Nick directly.

"I called and couldn't get anybody. I left a message." she said, "No one ever called me back."

The policy was simple. Court-ordered random urine screenings were just that—random, meaning that you were subject to being screened at any time, any day. Thus, you had to be available. Refusing to be screened or an excuse of any kind meant you were marked positive. Everyone knew and understood the procedure. Even Miss Collins.

"So, is this to say that you're not coming to the office?" Nick asked, not wanting to waste any more time.

"I can't," the other stated, "I said I got a job inter—"

"Okay, thank you, have a nice day." Nick said and walked back to the minivan. When he got in, he called Karen on his cell phone and conveyed the news.

"She's refusing?" Karen asked.

"'Fraid so," he stated, "Claims she's got a job interview today."

Karen sighed, "All right," she said, "Thanks anyway."

Back at the office, he finished some paperwork. Looking at his watch, Nick realized that it was nearing time to go home. The day had been so busy with paper, he thought, that the time had flown by.

He drove home and it dawned on him that he had not called or heard from Amy since he had left that morning. The summons to the doctor's office remained in the back of his mind, but still he had received no word from Amy—or her doctor, for that matter.

When he arrived home, Amy was sitting by the window, staring outside. He wanted to ask, but knew not to push. Upon seeing him, she walked over and kissed him. "How was your day?" she asked.

"Busy," he answered, "Yours?"

"Okay, I guess…" her voice trailed off.

"You *guess?*" he asked incredulously.

"Yeah," she answered, "I…*guess.*"

He looked at her, "Well?" he asked.

"Well, what?" she was teasing.

"C'mon," he said, "Spill it."

"Spill what?"

"The doctor," he intoned, "And what did she wanna see you about?"

"Oh, that."

"Yes…*that.*"

She took his hands in hers, looked him in the eyes, and said, "I'm free."

"You're *free?*" he asked, not following.

"Yes…I'm…*free!*"

"Meaning?" he asked further.

"Meaning," she said to him, "It's gone."

Nick still could not follow. "Huh? What? What's gone?"

"*It's* gone," she said, "The tumor…it's gone. I'm tumor-and cancer-free!"

There was a long pause. Finally Nick, at a loss for words, said, "I don't think that's funny if it's a joke!"

"Nick, it's *not* a joke!" Amy said, annoyance in her voice, "The doctor did some checking, searching, prodding…she found no sign of the tumor or anything! It's as if it was never even there!"

Nick had no idea how to respond. He was beyond happy, but lost in thought.

"Well?" the look on Amy's face snapped him back to real time.

"Well…" he answered, not knowing what else to say, "I love you honey…" he took her in his arms and held her tightly, while repeating in a low voice: *IloveyouIloveyouIloveyou*…

"I love you too!" replied Amy, matching her man's tone and volume.

■■

Family Service Specialist 1 Bob Hendrick, the LO's senior worker, announced his retirement. After 31 years with the Division, he was, in his own words, "hanging up the boxing gloves".

Many of his cases—he worked out of the Adolescent Unit—were being reassigned to FSS Trainee Angie Franconero. Poor Angie was going to have a shitload on her plate.

"But, hey, she's a vet," so went the reasoning, "She'd been overseas fightin' and kickin' ass for our country. She's tough, she'll be okay."

A retirement dinner was arranged at a restaurant, with drinks at the bar within. Workers, Unit Supervisors, and Case Work Sups from three LOs including Bob's own, attended. Also in attendance were the LO Managers from the respective offices, and Area Director Kathy Blasi.

Some of the attendees had even brought their spouses or significant others to the function. Nick was there, and he had brought Amy. His boss Karen and Amy were chatting up a storm.

Lisa Morales brought her husband; Bryan Taylor his wife; many of the other staff their respective partners yet chatting it up among each other. Shop talk—without divulging client names. Confidentiality forbidding such.

Nick, though enjoying the festivity, could not help but notice the emptiness in the room.

He chatted it up with Kim Burkett and Randy Spencer for a time, yet in their talking, all three had felt the void, yet unspoken. No one could miss it.

Paul was gone.

Fanny was gone.

Paulette was gone.

And now, Bob will be gone. Bob was—is—loved and respected just as much. Everyone was going to miss his gruff voice and rough-around-the-edges demeanor, which concealed his soft compassionate manner. The voice of a lion, the manner of a pussycat.

The job, Nick discerned, was a shark tank. *And sometimes I feel like a minnow swimming with the sharks, waiting to be devoured alive!*

■■

Arlene Rollins was discharged from the rehabilitation facility after her sixty-day inpatient program.

Her lawyer, in that time, had worked diligently in her favor; the possession charge was reduced to a disorderly conduct offense. Upon advise of her counsel, Arlene pleaded guilty to the amended and in lieu of jail time or community service, the judge imposed a $300 fine, plus court costs.

In a closed-door conference between herself, her Union representative, and LO Manager Marie Kovacs, discussions ensued. Given Arlene's overall good performance record as well as no past disfavorable notations in her personnel file, it was decided, per Employee Relations, that FSS Arlene Rollins be reinstated, with the written stipulation that she continue to attend AA/NA meetings and other ordered programs.

In addition, Arlene discovered, she was being reassigned to the Union West Local Office, at which she will continue her FSS duties.

Later that day, she met with her pastor and filled him in on the latest details. "I…almost feel…*reborn!*" she had said to him.

To which the pastor responded: "The power of prayer, my dear. Never stray from the power of prayer…if He brought you to it, He will bring you through it!"

Allied Moving Services was dispatched to haul Fanny Palumbo's personal effects to her parents' home in Pennsylvania.

Workers Compensation, Disability and other paperwork was filed on her behalf, and that, with her insurance, would net a good chunk of money—equivalent, if not slightly more than, her full salary, for the rest of her life.

Saying goodbye to the Division and her familiar resources was, in her mind, the most difficult thing she could ever do. Aware of her inability to fully function as a worker—as well as leaving her home to be cared for—Fanny took it very hard, and for a time was inconsolable.

The transition to her new environment went smoothly, as did the in-home and outpatient physical therapy. But, as all involved knew, it would be the emotional therapy that would be difficult.

Her mom and dad alternated in taking her to the therapy sessions, as Fanny could not drive. It was in one of the private meetings at which the dam had burst.

The therapist had asked her a series of intense questions about her life, her childhood, her educational and work history. All had gone well—Fanny had made friends over the years. She had done exceptionally well in grade school, high school, and college. She told the therapist, when asked, about her work history prior to her appointment to the Division.

She had seen many changes in her years in the Division, so she told the therapist. The good as well as the bad. However, when the talk slowly shifted to the event that ultimately changed her life, Fanny spoke easily at first but before she realized it, her voice was getting tight and its tone was changing. Seeing that crazy woman clearly in her mind as she tried to speak, Fanny's voice rose in volume as all the anger, sadness and helplessness within her unleashed.

She screamed her unhappiness and more than a few expletives dotted the tirade as her verbal eruption led to uncontrollable sobbing.

Mrs. Palumbo was waiting outside in the main room reading a magazine when she heard the unmistakable voice of her daughter. Dropping the magazine, she ran to the session room and burst in without knocking. Seeing her daughter, she rushed to comfort her as the other sat crying loudly. She said nothing, but glanced at the therapist—her glance conveying: *What have you done to my baby? Hasn't she been through enough?*

That evening, Mrs. Palumbo cornered her husband and insisted without negotiation that they find another therapist for Fanny.

It was expected that even with their insurance, the bills for Fanny's recovery would mount. It will be difficult, but somehow, they would take care of it all.

However, nary a bill was sent to the Palumbo home. Mr. Palumbo, after some time had passed, began to wonder why. He contacted the medical and therapy facilities and inquired about the billing status. "Sir," stated the head of accounts payable, "You have a zero balance. All of your daughter's visits and care have been paid for."

"How the hell can that be?" he inquired incredulously, "I never sent you any payment. Neither did my wife, for that matter."

"I don't know, sir," said the woman, "but as far as we're concerned, you owe us nothing."

He hung up and conveyed the information to his wife, who intoned, "Whadaya mean it's all paid? What the hell…?"

"I don't know," he said, holding up his hands, "Maybe a glitch in their billing system or something. Who the hell knows?"

What they *didn't* know was that all of

Fanny's therapy and care had been paid for anonymously—the anonymity being that of Dominick "Heavy Legs" Valenza, *sotto capo,* whose son and now-dead niece caused the pain and suffering of the now-disabled State worker.

That stupid niece of his created so much embarrassment that the State Police were now looking at the Family more closely. What's more, his own son was involved. *I'll take care a' that rat bastard,* he thought, *I'll cut his fuckin' legs an' balls off!*

He wished he could apologize to the Palumbos, but with the heat on so intensely, he felt that the least he could do is pay for that poor girl's care.

****

There was a bad feeling in the air.

Much as Nick and others around him tried to deny and shake it off, such could not be avoided.

He saw it in his colleagues' eyes: their look coupled with his own body language revealed the changes happening—the job had changed. Everyone had changed. *He* had changed, also.

He, like many others, had joined the

Division to help people, only to be more often than not ostracized, shunned and at times, ridiculed. He was never one to carry his work aggravation around like a satchel, but just yesterday, Amy, noticing his abnormal silence, worked on him diligently, insisting that he speak out and say what was on his mind.

And he, after endless prodding from she, finally did speak. Once begun, Nick was unable to stop, for the words spilled like Niagara Falls. And as the words fell, so eventually did his emotions.

Nick at first attempted to conceal his raw feelings, for he needed to show strength and not give in. Amy, not one to judge or criticize, held her man as the tears began to flow, and for a time Nick could not speak as he sobbed peacefully on her shoulder.

Let it out, she soothed him encouragingly, *Let it all out.*

And let it out he did, as he cried for those who suffered. And those who continued to suffer. He had seen more than his share.

After a short time, he composed himself and looked at Amy. "Tell me the truth," he asked directly, "Are you *really* okay?"

She knew what he meant. "Yes," she answered emphatically, "I've been back for a second, and even a third time. All confirmed.

Remission."

A few moments of silence followed, during which they and they alone enjoyed. The last tear wiped away indicating all troubles—professional, personal and otherwise—for the moment, forgotten.

■■

A new influx of workers was added to the Local Office.

Fresh off the Civil Service list, the newcomers consisted of 3 FSS Trainees, 2 AFSWs, 1 Unit Supervisor (just promoted), and a FSS2, reassigned from a South Jersey LO.

Nick, along with another veteran AFSW, Kim Burkett, was field training a couple of new workers after their introductions. Among others, they were shown the locations of the nearby maintenance facilities, at which the State vehicles are fueled, as well as the motor pool facilities and their contact numbers in the event of a breakdown on the road.

Back at the office, Nick, Kim, and the newbies engaged in friendly conversation, exchanging small bits of information here and there.

"Is this job as rough as I've heard?" one of the new workers asked. She was a young woman of twenty-four, recent NJIT graduate leaning towards social work rather than her Civil Engineering major.

"What *have* you heard?" asked Kim, looking at the young woman.

"Well…I heard a few stories here an' there…" said the trainee, "Just that, you know…people look at CPS workers as bad people…we go takin' kids an' stuff…"

"Um…" Kim cut in, "We don't just go *taking* anybody." Everyone else was quiet at this reply, "What we do is investigate and look for any signs of abuse, neglect, whatever. We speak with the child—or child*ren*, if more than one," she went on, "We also speak with anyone responsible for the safety of the child—parents, teachers, whomever. If any sign of abuse or neglect is found, or substantiated, then we do what needs to be done.

"Try and put yourself in the shoes of some child," Kim went on, speaking thickly, "We got parents who are druggies, parents who're locked up, parents who don't give a damn about anyone but themselves—they don't even give a damn about their own *child,* someone they conceived and brought into this world…"

The others looked on, listening. Nick shot Kim a look, as if to say: *You're right about the parents, but what about the caregivers? What about the courts? What about the bosses? Do you really think* anyone *gives a damn?*

He had heard it all before; he had even preached the same sermon early in his career.

Now he knew better. It was not as simple as it's said. As experience has taught him and many others, there was no black or white— only a million different shades of gray.

And the new trainees, in time, will endure their own battles, as did Nick and the others. And as Kim went on speaking, Nick thought of the comrades he'd known that were no longer.

Each of whom had paid a price far beyond value. It was only a matter of time as to who else would be sucked into that unforgiving vortex.

■■

Fire departments from five towns were dispatched to a multi-alarmer at an industrial center near Perth Amboy. The blaze and smoke could be seen for miles in all directions; it would be hours before the fire could be put under control.

Only after the area was washed down and cleared of any smoldering embers did the State fire marshals conduct their investigation. It was upon such that a body was discovered, charred beyond recognition. The remains were loaded into a County Medical Examiner's truck to be taken to the morgue for identification—if possible.

It was later determined through dental records that the remains were those of one James "Jimmy V" Valenza, son of the reputed *sotto capo*.

Jimmy V, it was later reported, had just been released from jail on $750,000 bail. It was suspected that the fire was intentional.

Upon hearing the news of his son's tragic demise, "Heavy Legs" sobbed openly and loudly, "My boy," he cried, and the tears flowed like a waterfall as his words broke, "My…boy…he's…g-o-o-onnne…" and he could say no more.

Only he knew that those tears shed were crocodile tears, for his "poor, departed boy" had caused him much embarrassment and grief while on this Earth.

Eighteen months later Nick was dressing himself at home, preparing to go to work. He had donned a maroon dress shirt coupled with soft tan slacks, topped off with a medium grey windbreaker jacket.

He turned slowly, to let Amy assess his appearance. "What do y' think?" he asked.

"I think," she answered, "that that's a handsome man standing before me!" They both laughed.

"Still can't believe it," she said, "Nick Donovan, Residential Coordinator!"

He had been offered a position at a residential treatment facility. Regular hours, better pay and health benefits. Although it was hard to say goodbye to the Division, Nick knew that he had to keep climbing, keep moving forward. The director of the residential facility, knowing Nick and his background, worked diligently to steal a good man away from the Division.

Although he already knew the terrain on which he was treading, Nick was still a bit nervous. "You sure I look all right?" he asked for what had to be the twenty-second time.

"Baby," Amy asserted, "you look fine. Now get out there and knock 'em dead! They know that you're a good one."

And within that year, as changes happen, Nick remained in contact with many of his former colleagues and bosses within the Division. He still missed Paul, but secured himself with the knowledge that Paul was in a better place, and no longer suffering.

As was his Amy, who was now Mrs. Nick Donovan!

***

ABOUT THE AUTHOR

Eric A. Mouzon is a former Child Protective Services worker. He worked in the Social Services field for over 25 years as a Youth Mentor, Youth Group Worker, and Family Service Worker. His first book, *Vietnam on the Hudson,* was a true story about life in a children's residential care facility.
Mr. Mouzon has worked with at-risk children and families, and in his career has undergone a vast variety of experiences in the field. He lives in New Jersey.